# YELLOWSTONE

## Marjorie Benson

Biological Consultant

**Dr. Evelyn Merrill**
College of Natural Resources
University of Wisconsin, Stevens Point

**RAINTREE
STECK-VAUGHN**
P U B L I S H E R S
The Steck-Vaughn Company

*Austin, Texas*

**A production of B&B Publishing, Inc.**

**Editor** – Jean B. Black
**Photo Editor** – Margie Benson
**Computer Specialist** – Katy O'Shea
**Interior Design** – Scott Davis

**Raintree Steck-Vaughn Publishing Staff**

**Project Editor** – Helene Resky
**Project Manager** – Joyce Spicer

LIBRARY OF CONGRESS CATALOGING-IN-PUBLICATION DATA

Benson, Marjorie.
    Yellowstone / by Marjorie Benson
        p. cm. — (Wonders of the world)
    Includes bibliographical references (p.) and index.
    ISBN 0-8114-6365-8
    1. Yellowstone National Park — Juvenile Literature. 2. Natural History — Yellowstone National Park — Juvenile Literature. [1. Yellowstone National Park. 2. Natural history—Yellowstone National Park. 3. National parks and reserves.] I. Title. II. Series.
F722.B45 1995                        94-34461
978.7'52 — dc20                CIP  AC

Cover photo
**Riverside Geyser on the banks of Firehole River**

Title page photo
**Pearl Geyser, Lower Geyser Basin**

Table of Contents page photo
**A bull moose crosses the Lewis River in Yellowstone National Park.**

# PHOTO SOURCES

Cover Photo: © Greg Probst Photography

© Jeff and Alexa Henry: 1, 13 bottom, 25 left, 40 left
© Gary Kramer: 42 left
© Dr. Alan K. Mallams: 3, 7 bottom, 9 right, 39, 41 top, 46 both, 49 left, 53 right
National Park Service photo by W. S. Keller: 14 top, 41 left
National Park Service photo by Cecil W. Stroughton: 55
© Fred Siskind: 4, 5, 10 left, 11 top, 12, 13 right, 14 bottom, 17 right, 18, 19 left, 20, 23 top, 24, 26 top, 28, 29 all, 30 top, 31 both, 32 both, 33 top, 34, 35 left, 36, 37 top, 45 bottom, 47 bottom, 52 bottom, 56, 60 right, 61 both

Targhee National Forest: 15 left, 42 right, 49 right, 50 top right, 50 top left, 58 both, 59 left, 60 left
U. S. Fish and Wildlife Service photo by Bob Benke: 47 top
U. S. Fish and Wildlife Service photo by Chris Servheen: 43
U. S. Fish and Wildlife Service photo by Ralph Town: 7 right
© Barbara von Hoffman: 30 left
Yellowstone National Park: 9 bottom, 16, 17 left, 19 top, 21 both, 22, 23 right, 35 right, 38 right, 48, 50 left, 51, 52 left, 53 left, 54 both, 57 both, 59 right
Yellowstone National Park photo by Marsha Karle: 6, 10 bottom, 25 right, 26 bottom, 33 right, 35 top, 44 both

Printed and bound in the United States of America.
1 2 3 4 5 6 7 8 9 VH 99 98 97 96 95 94

# Table of Contents

# Chapter One

# A Natural High

Almost every visitor to Yellowstone National Park waits to see Old Faithful Geyser erupt (left).

A modern highway leads another family in their van toward the exit ramp marked "Old Faithful." Traveling on blacktop all the way from Jackson Hole, Wyoming, they have made good time.

Pulling into the Old Faithful complex, the family spots an empty parking place near the cafeteria and post office. The crowds are much bigger than they expected, almost like shopping mall crowds at Christmas. A large poster outside the visitors' center boldly predicts "Time of Next Old Faithful Eruption: 1:52." The father checks his watch—it's 1:47. They have to hurry; no time now for a quick look inside the historic Old Faithful Inn.

Squeezing past dogs on leashes, toddlers, backpackers, and tourists from Germany, the young family occupies the last front-row space on a wooden bench. As they sit, eyes focused on the slightly raised mound in front of them, 1:53 passes, 1:54, and nothing happens. Suddenly, a puff of white steam floats from the center of the chalky mound, followed by a spasm of bubbling water gurgling from the geyser's opening. Hundreds of cameras spring into place as if an automatic signal triggered them. Water spouts 10 to 20 feet (3 m to 6 m) into the air in the next few seconds—and a brief wave of disappointment fills the air as the people think, "That's it?"

And then it happens. The geyser they all came to see shoots a watery column skyward with a low, powerful roar. Today is an exceptional day—there is no wind. Old Faithful climbs 180 feet (55 m) in just 20 seconds.

As suddenly as it began, the entire eruption is over. In less than five minutes, what everyone traveled miles to see is gone. The young family takes one last picture in front of the "Old Faithful Geyser" sign. If they hurry, they can make it to Cody, Wyoming, by dark. On the way, they'll be able to see Yellowstone Lake from the comfort of their van.

Today, over three million visitors drive through the park's five entrances every year. Most of them travel the 142-mile (228-km) Grand Loop Highway. Almost everyone stops at the park's enduring attraction, Old Faithful Geyser. Only a few venture beyond to experience the entire Upper Geyser Basin and the

Built in the 1930s, Old Faithful Inn is only a short walk from Old Faithful Geyser.

Grand Geyser may shoot water up to 200 feet (61 m) high, but it is not as regular as Old Faithful. There are at least 6 hours between eruptions.

rest of its geysers and hot springs. Just north of Old Faithful Inn, Grand Geyser, the tallest predictable geyser in the world, reaches a height of 200 feet (61 m)—but few have time to wait and watch. And even fewer hike to such places as Shoshone Geyser Basin where Union Geyser spouts from three vents at the same time.

## No Equal on Earth

It was to the Upper Geyser Basin that Henry D. Washburn, surveyor general of the Territory of Montana, and his military escort, Lt. Gustavus C. Doane, came in September of 1870. As their expedition emerged from the pine forest surrounding Old Faithful, the geyser greeted them with a grand eruption. Awestruck, Lt. Doane recorded, "The earth affords not its equal. It is the most lovely inanimate object in existence." In less than 24 hours, these early Yellowstone visitors were overwhelmed— 12 geysers in the Upper Basin erupted in a thermal wonder show. Appreciation for all they saw and felt led these men to campaign effectively for a new kind of public park.

In 1872, an act of Congress made their vision reality. Yellowstone National Park became the first national park in the world. It was known simply as "public park" then, but people called it "Yellowstone" so often that the title later became official. The name came from the golden bluffs of the Yellowstone River that lie beyond the park's northern boundary.

By establishing a national park, the United States began a tradition of setting aside unique natural areas. This conservation idea was relatively new in the 1870s, and it spread to all parts of the world. Today, Yellowstone is the most famous national park on Earth, but few visitors really experience it. Washburn and Doane spent a day and a half in the Upper Geyser Basin. Most modern visitors might spend an hour or two near Old Faithful. One early visitor to the park, unhappy with the coming of cars in 1915, said it all: "Nothing can be done well at a speed of 40 miles (64 km) a day." Today, only a few slow down enough to realize how unique Yellowstone National Park is.

## Inside the Mountains

Within a protective wall of eleven mountain ranges, Yellowstone National Park covers an area of 2,219,823 acres (898,714 ha) in northwest Wyoming, spreading into Idaho and Montana. Packed within those acres are countless natural features, colors, and contrasts—plants, animals, mountains, valleys, canyons, grasslands, forests, hot springs, lakes, rivers, waterfalls, and geysers. Everything seems to interact perfectly in every season of the year.

Lodgepole pines, spruce, aspen, Douglas fir, and other trees and plants blanket the high plateaus in every shade of green. Burned forests of brown and black contrast with new undergrowth and flower-sprinkled meadows nearby. Every kind and color of wildflower blooms here—red monkey flowers, purple gentian, yellow balsamroot, blue Alpine forget-me-nots. Specially adapted microscopic plants, called algae and bacteria, live in the hot springs. Clear water bubbles in cauldrons of orange, brown, yellow, and pink.

Grizzly bears, black bears, and one of the largest elk herds in the United States live in the meadows and forests. Mule deer, moose, and bison drink from calm, clear waterways. Bighorn sheep scramble over the craggy peaks. The park hosts trumpeter swans, white pelicans, and bald eagles.

Moose are a common sight in the meadows and near the waterways of Yellowstone.

The Gallatin Range, with many peaks over 10,000 feet (3,408 m), towers above grazing elk at Swan Lake Flats. These mountains extend from Bozeman, Montana, into the northwest portion of Yellowstone.

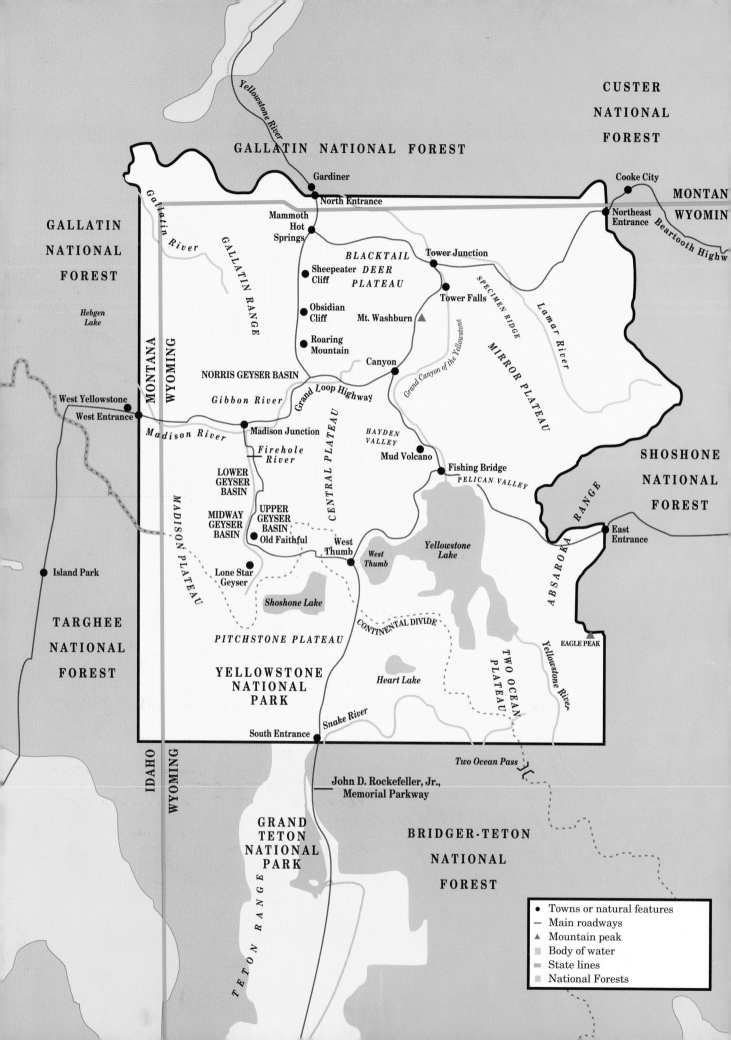

CUSTER
NATIONAL
FOREST

GALLATIN NATIONAL FOREST

*Yellowstone River*

Gardiner

Cooke City

North Entrance

MONTAN
WYOMIN

GALLATIN
NATIONAL
FOREST

Mammoth
Hot
Springs

Northeast
Entrance

*Beartooth Highw*

*Gallatin River*

*Hebgen
Lake*

GALLATIN RANGE

Sheepeater
Cliff

BLACKTAIL *DEER*
*PLATEAU*

Tower Junction

*SPECIMEN RIDGE*

*Lamar River*

MONTANA
WYOMING

Obsidian
Cliff

Mt. Washburn ▲

Tower Falls

MIRROR PLATEAU

Roaring
Mountain

NORRIS GEYSER BASIN

*Gibbon River*

Canyon

*Grand Canyon of the Yellowstone*

*Grand Loop Highway*

West Yellowstone

West Entrance

Madison Junction

HAYDEN
VALLEY

*Madison River*

*Firehole
River*

CENTRAL PLATEAU

Mud Volcano

Fishing Bridge

*PELICAN VALLEY*

SHOSHONE
NATIONAL
FOREST

LOWER
GEYSER
BASIN

MIDWAY
GEYSER
BASIN

UPPER
GEYSER
BASIN
Old Faithful

West
Thumb

*West
Thumb*

*Yellowstone
Lake*

*MADISON PLATEAU*

Lone Star
Geyser

East
Entrance

Island Park

*Shoshone Lake*

*ABSAROKA RANGE*

TARGHEE
NATIONAL
FOREST

PITCHSTONE PLATEAU

CONTINENTAL DIVIDE

EAGLE PEAK ▲

*Yellowstone River*

YELLOWSTONE
NATIONAL
PARK

*Heart Lake*

TWO OCEAN
PLATEAU

*Snake River*

South Entrance

IDAHO
WYOMING

*Two Ocean Pass*

John D. Rockefeller, Jr.,
Memorial Parkway

*TETON RANGE*

GRAND
TETON
NATIONAL
PARK

BRIDGER-TETON
NATIONAL
FOREST

● Towns or natural features
— Main roadways
▲ Mountain peak
▮ Body of water
▬ State lines
▮ National Forests

# The Forces of Nature

In a place so mountainous, so green, and so full of life, it is hard to imagine that Yellowstone was once part of a huge, lifeless plain located near the equator. Oceans of warm, shallow water covered that barren land. Over millions of years, the waters came and went repeatedly. Tiny shelled animals died, their remains becoming grainy sediment. This material was laid down, layer upon layer, forming a rock called limestone. Other types of sediment, such as clay, sand, and mud, formed sandstone, shale, and other sedimentary rocks. Slowly and quietly, a rocky foundation was laid.

To comprehend what happened next, we need to understand what geologists call plate tectonics. This theory states that the Earth's outer shell is made up of about 12 floating plates that bump and push against each other. For example, South America is on one plate, and North America on another. When these plates collide, the Earth's crust rises, falls, or folds. Earthquakes and volcanoes relieve the stress.

About 100 million years ago, the North American plate began approaching the Pacific plate. Scientists believe that the Pacific plate actually moved under the North American plate, resulting in a volcanic period. It also caused the mountain ranges of western North America near Yellowstone to begin to rise.

The Yellowstone region itself experienced a period of heavy volcanic activity about 50 million years ago. Most of these eruptions were fairly quiet, with rivers of slow-moving lava flowing from volcanoes,

Tower Falls drops 132 feet (40 m) into Tower Creek. Many waterfalls in Yellowstone were formed from lava flows that were resistant to erosion.

## FOSSIL FORESTS

Yellowstone's fossil forests are another reminder of its volcanic history. These stone trees, many of them still standing upright, cover 24.5 square miles (64 sq km). The best examples are located on the ridges above Lamar Valley. On Specimen Ridge and below Amethyst Mountain, 27 distinct forest layers have been identified.

About 50 million years ago, periods of volcanism alternated with periods of relative calm. During the calm periods, forests grew to maturity; during the volcanic periods, these forests were buried in fine volcanic ash and debris. This volcanic debris contained a mineral called silica. Rivers and streams, clogged with debris, changed course, flowing over buried forests. This surface water and other subsurface groundwater carried dissolved silica that began to petrify the buried tree stumps. Silica seeped in to fill the open spaces around the wood cells, eventually turning the wood into hard quartz. As volcanic activity died down, conditions became favorable for new forest growth. Later volcanic periods came and went as the petrified forest layers multiplied. Most of Yellowstone's fossilized trees are hardwoods such as dogwood, maple, and oak, indicating that the climate used to be much warmer.

or cracks in the Earth's crust. This type of lava is called andesite and forms fine-grained, gray rock.

Then, about two million years ago, a different kind of violent volcanism occurred. A huge bubble of magma, or melted rock, about 60 miles (95 km) wide swelled up from the Earth's crust and exploded. A huge cloud of ash, debris, and air suspended in the magma, called a pyroclastic flow, was thrown out and moved at very high speed. When it stopped, the small pieces of ash and debris fused together immediately, forming a type of volcanic rock called welded tuff. The main ingredient of this rock is rhyolite, a light-colored material full of silica, the mineral from which glass is made. Rhyolite is not usually found on the surface of the Earth, but Yellowstone is literally buried in it—1,600 square miles (4,140 sq km) of rhyolite reach down to a depth of 1,000 feet (300 m).

With pressure from the magma gone, the volcanic crater collapsed, forming a huge depression called a caldera. Most of this caldera cannot be identified today, but parts of its ancient rim can be seen along the park's southern boundary.

Scientists believe a second big eruption occurred about 600,000 years after the first, creating a smaller caldera about 18 miles (30 km) across. It is located near Island Park, Idaho, along the western boundary of the park.

A third gigantic eruption occurred 600,000 years ago. A huge mile-deep caldera was left behind. Yellowstone Lake now occupies a small portion of this ancient depression, and most of the park's Central Plateau lies within it.

The basalt columns of Sheepeater Cliff near Bunsen Peak were formed when volcanic lava contracted as it cooled.

One of the world's largest calderas, measuring 28 miles by 47 miles (45 km by 76 km), lies within the park. Yellowstone Lake (bottom) occupies part of this ancient caldera.

# CANYONS OF THE YELLOWSTONE RIVER

Beginning south of the park high in the Bridger-Teton National Forest, the Yellowstone River is the last of the great rivers in the United States untouched by dams or other river control projects. Sixteen miles (26 km) after the river flows from

Yellowstone Lake, it becomes a geologic showcase. Falling 109 feet (33 m) at Upper Falls, the water races on to the second most popular sight in the park—Lower Falls. Here the river drops 308 feet (94 m) into the Grand Canyon of the Yellowstone. This magnificent 21-mile- ( 35-km- ) long gorge—1,500 to 4,000 feet (455 m to 1,220 m) wide and 1,200 feet (366 m) deep—was carved over thousands of years by running water from melting glaciers. At the top of the canyon, ancient lava cooled, forming six-sided basalt columns bunched together like giant building blocks. Most visitors, however, notice the bright colors of the canyon walls below. Rhyolite rock is usually light gray or brown, but these rocky cliffs have been baked by hot steam and gases escaping from deep below the surface. Oxides of various minerals in the rhyolite have tinted the surface brilliant orange and yellow. Miles beyond this colorful canyon, the river receives the waters of the Lamar River before entering the less colorful Black Canyon of the Yellowstone. Few visitors even know about this 10-mile- (16-km-) long volcanic gorge where cougars and bighorn sheep live.

Other less violent volcanic activity continued, with lava oozing and cooling for thousands of years to create Yellowstone's plateaus. The rhyolite that forms Pitchstone Plateau is only 80,000 years old.

So much volcanic activity taking place in such a small area is very unusual. Earth's crust is about 25 miles (40 km) thick in most places, but in Yellowstone it is very thin. Some scientists believe a huge ocean of super-hot magma lies only 2 to 6 miles (3.2 to 9.7 km) beneath the surface. Yellowstone is what scientists call a "hot spot." At a depth of 200 feet (60 m), the temperature is 300°F (149°C). This heat fuels the thermal (hot water) features—geysers, hot springs, mud pots, and steam vents.

Cold also shaped this special place. Between the volcanic eras, thick glaciers carved the landscape. There have been four distinct ice ages spanning 100,000 years, the last one ending 12,500 years ago. During these periods, mountains were sharpened, canyons scooped out, and valleys formed.

The combined volcanic and glacial forces molded the area we now call Yellowstone. There are 32 mountains in the park over 10,000 feet (3,050 m) high and six peaks over 11,000 feet (3,350 m) high. Eagle Peak at 11,360 feet (3,463 m) is the highest. Yellowstone's seven high volcanic plateaus are not craggy mountains, but at an average elevation of 8,000 feet (2,440 m), they are higher than many mountain ranges.

**The peaks of the Grand Tetons in Wyoming near Yellowstone show how glaciers carved the craggy peaks.**

## Still Changing

The natural forces that created Yellowstone's high mountains and plateaus are still at work. There are no active lava flows today, but the huge ocean of magma is still thought to lie beneath the surface. Geysers still spout, springs still boil, and the Earth still moves frequently.

Ferdinand V. Hayden, head of the U.S. Geological Survey and leader of an expedition to Yellowstone in 1871, made reference to the earthquakes in the region. He wrote, "I have no doubt that if this part of the country should ever be settled and careful observations made, it would be found that earthquake shocks are of very common occurrence."

Hayden was right. Between 15 and 18 earthquakes are felt each year, making Yellowstone one of the Earth's major earthquake centers. In addition, thousands of "microquakes" that cannot be felt also cause the ground to shift.

On August 17, 1959, an earthquake measuring 7.1 on the Richter scale shook the Yellowstone region. (By comparison, the Los Angeles earthquake of January 17, 1994, measured 6.6 on the Richter scale.) Centered west of the park, the 1959 quake shook the region with the force of 200 atomic bombs. Water behind the dam at Hebgen Lake sloshed over the walls of the dam and rushed down the Madison

The view from the top of Mt. Washburn down into Hayden Valley looks peaceful and calm.

River Canyon. A new lake, Quake Lake, was formed by huge rock slides that built a natural dam across the canyon. Outside the park, 28 people died, covered with tons of rock at a campground. Inside the park, rock slides cut off sections of the Grand Loop Highway, and guests streamed out of the Old Faithful Inn.

The quake caused underground changes as well. A total of 298 geysers and hot springs erupted. For more than half of them, it was the first recorded eruption. Water temperatures in the thermal areas rose 6°F (3.4°C). The day after the quake, Sapphire Pool, a clear hot spring, began filling up with muddy water. Four weeks later it became an active geyser, shooting water 125 feet (38 m) into the air. These eruptions were so powerful that 100-pound (45-kg) pieces of geyserite—the rock that lines geysers inside and is deposited on the ground outside—were torn away and thrown skyward. The eruptions ended in 1964, and by 1971, the muddy water had become a beautiful sapphire blue again.

The Hebgen quake made geologists even more anxious to study Yellowstone. In 1984, they discovered that the Earth's crust was bulging beneath Yellowstone Lake. Some predicted the area was "heading toward another major ash-flow eruption," which would be a "major human disaster." But the unpredictable "bulge" began to deflate in 1991.

Earthquakes often cause changes in thermal activity. Clear springs and pools can become as muddy as the mud pots near Mud Volcano.

After the Hebgen quake of 1959, Clepsydra Geyser erupted continuously without a break.

# Today's Travelers

Change is the one true constant in Yellowstone National Park. The same ancient forces that shaped this corner of the world continue to rearrange it. Although humans do not have the power to make mountains or to create plateaus, they still have dramatically influenced life on Yellowstone's lands.

Many visitors enjoy fishing in the clear water of high mountain lakes.

In the following pages, our journey will take us through the park from early times to recent crises. We will concentrate on how beautiful the park is today and how it has survived in spite of increasing human activity. In 1885, John Muir called Yellowstone the "dwelling place of angels." We can only hope that both nature and people will spare this small piece of heaven on Earth for future generations to treasure.

Every visitor becomes a wildlife photographer at Yellowstone National Park. Here visitors photograph bison at Gibbon Meadow.

# Chapter Two

# Humans and Yellowstone

Archaeological evidence suggests that the Yellowstone region was used by humans for thousands of years—long before the Shoshone, Crow, or Blackfoot peoples migrated to the region. These early humans hunted animals and gathered plants for food. They mined obsidian for use in making weapons and tools. Their numbers were probably not very large for several reasons. The high mountains have few passes to let people into the region. In addition, temperatures in the long, cold winters can fall to -66°F (-54°C). Up to 15 feet (4.6 m) of snow covers the very high country most of the year. Lodgepole pine forests, clogged with fallen logs and debris, have always made travel very difficult. And hunting has never been easy in the high plateau regions of Yellowstone.

Rock paintings suggest that humans lived in the Yellowstone region thousands of years ago.

## Native Americans

In the late 1700s and 1800s, various Native American groups began moving farther west as white settlers came from the East. The Crow, Blackfoot, and Shoshone peoples traveled and settled in the lands surrounding Yellowstone. Food was fairly easy to obtain in the areas outside the present-day park.

The Crow lived in the Yellowstone River Valley and along its tributaries. They were good hunters who treasured their horses. For special occasions, they often decorated clothing with elk eyeteeth. The Blackfoot lived just east of Crow territory. They were an aggressive people who excelled in combat. Some Native Americans, as well as early trappers, feared this group and tried to avoid them. The Shoshone lived to the south, east, and west of what is now Yellowstone. They were probably the first group in the region to have horses.

Of the different groups living near Yellowstone, only one group actually lived within the park's boundaries. Known as the Tukudiaka, or Sheepeaters, they were related to the Shoshone. This small group probably entered Yellowstone near 1800,

Heavy snowstorms in the Yellowstone region make it difficult for bison and other animals to find enough food during the winter.

# COLTER'S HELL

In 1803, the United States paid France $15 million for the land that would later become many western states. Meriwether Lewis and William Clark left to explore this Louisiana Purchase in 1806. They took a northerly route that bypassed Yellowstone. John Colter, a trapper and mountain man who had been with their expedition, left Lewis and Clark in 1807 after meeting Manuel Lisa, a Missouri trader.

Lisa wanted to build trading posts in the Yellowstone region. Colter accepted the task of taking that news to the Native Americans. He came back from his journey full of stories about a strange place of geysers, hot springs, a huge lake, and giant petrified fish. No one believed him, and his find was laughingly labeled "Colter's Hell."

When the disheartened trapper saw Clark again in 1810, he recounted his earlier travels. Clark believed his former colleague and traced Colter's travel route through eastern and central Yellowstone on his 1814 map. Thus, Colter became the official discoverer of Yellowstone.

settling in the caves and among the rocks of the Washburn and Absaroka ranges. Their lean-to shelters, called wickiups, were made from branches and leaves. They had no horses or firearms, and were a peace-loving group whose main food supply was bighorn sheep. Trappers who passed through Yellowstone found these people to be friendly and helpful. They traded with the trappers and often gave them advice on where to find beavers. They also

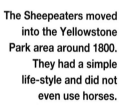

The Sheepeaters moved into the Yellowstone Park area around 1800. They had a simple life-style and did not even use horses.

shared the land with other Native American groups who passed through during the summer. After Yellowstone National Park was created, most of the Sheepeaters moved to one of several reservations in Idaho and Wyoming where other Shoshone lived.

## Trappers, Miners, and Explorers

Although trappers and traders made numerous trips across Colter's Hell, the rest of the world remained largely unaware of Yellowstone. Most of these explorers were unable to read and write, and people paid little attention to their "tall tales."

There was one exception, however. An educated trapper named Osborne Russell made five trips to Yellowstone and recorded his impressions. In his book, *Journal of a Trapper, 1834-43,* he wrote about the beautiful Lamar Valley, his favorite place, as it was in 1835: "We stopped at this place and for my own part I almost wished I could spend the remainder of my days in a place like this, where happiness and contentment seemed to reign in wild, romantic splendor, surrounded by majestic battlements which seemed to support the heavens and shut out all hostile intruders."

The Lamar River Valley located in northeastern Yellowstone is as beautiful today as it was when early trappers passed through. Herds of bison are seen near the upper Lamar River in the summer.

The stories of mountain man Jim Bridger motivated the government to find out, once and for all, if there really was such a place as Yellowstone. It was not a high priority, however. Of 110 exploratory expeditions sponsored by the government prior to 1859, only one went to Yellowstone.

The leader of the Yellowstone expedition was Captain W. F. Raynolds of the Corps of Topographical Engineers. With Jim Bridger as guide, the group left Fort Pierre, South Dakota, on April 13, 1859. They tried to pass through the Absaroka Range in June, but the snow was still too deep.

## JIM BRIDGER

The most famous of Yellowstone's early trappers was Jim Bridger. Born in Richmond, Virginia, in 1804, he was working for the Rocky Mountain Fur Company as a respected guide and explorer by 1822. Bridger had a remarkable ability to find any location without the aid of a printed map. He was also a great storyteller and exaggerated often in the telling of his tales. Bridger knew that most people thought his true stories were lies anyway, so why not make them even more entertaining!

A trapping party he led between 1841 and 1844 took Bridger to most areas of Yellowstone. He told of a place in the northeast part of Yellowstone that was dreary and lifeless (we now call it Specimen Ridge). A Crow chief had cursed this place. "Yes, siree, thar's miles o' peetrefied hills, covered with layers o' peetrefied trees, and on 'em trees ar peetrefied birds a singin' peetrefied songs!"

His "mountain of glass" story was also a favorite. Bridger tried to shoot an elk one day, and to his astonishment, the animal didn't fall. He shot again several times before approaching the elk, planning to bludgeon the animal with the butt of his rifle. Instead, he walked into a solid glass wall that was also a perfect telescope. The elk was actually 25 miles (40 km) away on the other side of a glass mountain now known as Obsidian Cliff.

Instead of going on, the captain turned north toward Canada to document the eclipse of the sun on July 29, 1859. "The valley of the Upper Yellowstone is yet a terra-incognita [unknown land], and we were compelled to content ourselves with listening to marvelous tales of burning plains, immense lakes, and boiling springs, without being able to verify these wonders." Raynolds' map of the region remained a blank space encircled by mountains.

When gold was discovered in California in 1848, miners fanned out over the West looking for another strike. Some came to the Yellowstone region in the 1860s and saw many of the wonders the trappers had seen. However, these men were better able to communicate what they saw, and interest in Yellowstone was renewed.

The Folsom-Cook-Peterson expedition traveled up the beautiful Madison River Valley.

Around this time, a group of prominent men from Virginia City, Montana, became interested in what the locals now called "Wonderland." Tired of waiting for a large expedition to go, David Folsom, Charles Cook, and William Peterson left Virginia City on September 6, 1863. Traveling up the Yellowstone River to Yellowstone Lake, they turned west and followed the Madison River Valley to their original departure point, a journey that took 36 days. They were amply rewarded with the wonders of the Grand Canyon of the Yellowstone, geyser basins, and Yellowstone Lake. But upon returning, these men were afraid to discuss what they had seen. Nathaniel P. Langford, a later explorer, wrote, "Bewildered and astounded at the marvels they beheld, they were, on their return, unwilling to risk their reputations for veracity by a full recital of them to a small company whom their friends had assembled to hear the account of their explorations."

## The National Park Idea

Cook, Folsom, and Peterson did manage, however, to convince Surveyor General Washburn of Montana that Bridger's tales were based on fact. Washburn and Lt. Doane led an official government expedition, leaving Fort Ellis on August 22, 1870. They followed the route of the Folsom-Cook-Peterson expedition along the banks of the Upper Yellowstone River.

All went well until the party was exploring the south side of Yellowstone Lake. Truman Everts, a

Belgian Pool in Upper Geyser Basin is only one of hundreds.

former tax agent, became separated from the main group. His horse took flight along with everything needed for Everts' survival in this wilderness, including his gun, blankets, and matches. For the next 37 days, Everts wandered through Yellowstone country alone—with just a pair of opera glasses and two knives. He managed to stay warm in the chilly September weather by lying on the warm ground near a small hot spring. He lived on cooked roots and grasses. The Washburn party spent seven days searching for Everts but had to abandon their efforts when their own food supplies became dangerously low.

The expedition moved on, saddened by the loss of Everts. As they came through the pine forest, Old Faithful erupted in full grandeur. That same day the men discovered and named Grand, Lion, Giantess, Castle, and Splendid geysers. Hot-water pools in a rainbow of colors were christened Rainbow, Morning Glory, Topaz, Sapphire, and Emerald.

The next night, September 19, the group camped where the Firehole and Gibbon rivers meet. That day they had passed more thermal features in the Lower Geyser Basin than they had time to explore or name. Some writers suggest that while the group discussed how they could profit from Yellowstone's wonders, Cornelius Hedges, an attorney and reporter, spoke up. He thought private ownership of any of these wonders was wrong—a region as unique as this deserved protection from profit. The men talked for hours about setting aside a national park where all citizens could experience what they had. Years earlier, artist George Catlin had suggested that everything west of the Mississippi be conserved as a huge "nation's park." Hedges' idea, however, was much more limited. He thought Yellowstone's major thermal features could be fenced off for the public.

The Washburn expedition camped near Firehole River.

Upon returning from their trip, members of the expedition became zealous missionaries for the national park idea. Lt. Doane finished his official report on December 15, 1870, and sent it to General Tecumseh Sherman, who enthusiastically passed the report to members of Congress.

Everts was finally rescued by two men sent back to Yellowstone after the Washburn expedition had already returned home. Down to just 50 pounds (23 kg), he was frostbitten, scalded, and unable to walk. However, despite his severe ordeal, Everts fully recovered.

Nathaniel P. Langford published a series of articles in Scribner's and the Overland Monthly about the expedition and gave lectures in the nation's largest cities. His story of the miraculous survival of Truman Everts heightened the interest of the entire nation.

Dr. Ferdinand V. Hayden, head of the U.S. Geological Survey of the Territories, had traveled with Bridger in 1859. He formed an official government expedition in 1871 whose purpose was to document the Yellowstone region. Photographer William Jackson and artist Thomas Moran, as well as a team of 19 scientists, left Fort Ellis near Bozeman, Montana, on July 15, 1871. Lt. Doane again led the military escort. Every detail of Yellowstone was cataloged, mapped, photographed, sketched, and measured. When this expedition returned with its evidence, Congress was ready to act.

The Yellowstone River winds through Hayden Valley, named after Ferdinand V. Hayden, who led several expeditions to the Yellowstone region in the 1870s. Publicity about his work in Yellowstone led to the creation of Yellowstone National Park in 1872.

On December 18, 1871, a Montana congressman named William Clagett put forth the National Park Act. It was signed into law by President Ulysses S. Grant on March 1, 1872. The land near the headwaters of the Yellowstone River was "reserved and withdrawn from settlement, occupancy, or sale...and dedicated and set apart as a public park or pleasuring ground for the benefit and enjoyment of the people...regulations shall provide for the preservation from injury or spoliation of all timber, mineral deposits, natural curiosities, or wonders within said park, and their retention in their natural condition."

## Managing the Park

On May 10, 1872, N.P., or "National Park," Langford was appointed the park's first superintendent. He was given no salary, no budget, and no real authority. The idea of a national park and how to preserve it was not well developed.

Small groups guided by mountain men thought of a visit to Yellowstone as a big hunting or fishing trip. Professional hunters came to the park to slaughter wildlife. Elk hides brought $8 apiece, and bison heads were worth $400. In 1876, a park visitor, General William Strong, wrote, "...few years will elapse before every elk, mountain sheep, and deer will have been killed, or driven from the mountains and valleys of the national park.... How is it that the Commissioner of the Park allows this unlawful killing?"

The first superintendent of Yellowstone National Park was Nathaniel P. Langford.

In 1877, Philetus Norris of Michigan was appointed park superintendent and given $10,000 to construct trails, bridges, and campgrounds. In 1880, he appointed Harry Yount game warden, but Yount later resigned because the job was too big for one man. This was wilderness, and visitors wanted no restraints. Even government officials didn't support conservation. In 1883, Hoke Smith, secretary of the interior, caught 200 trout in just one day.

In 1883, a short side track of the Northern Pacific Railroad ended at Cinnabar, near Gardiner, Montana. Transportation into the park was by stagecoach or on horseback. About 5,000 tourists came to the park every year. They climbed over the geyser cones, hacking off souvenir pieces. They

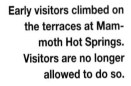

Early visitors climbed on the terraces at Mammoth Hot Springs. Visitors are no longer allowed to do so.

carved their names in hot spring basins. There were amusement rides, bears on chains, toll bridges, pens of elk—and plenty of people selling refreshments and souvenirs.

General Philip H. Sheridan, a Civil War hero, was instrumental in saving the park from mismanagement. Beginning in 1881, he visited Yellowstone every year and reported to the public on the condition of Yellowstone's wildlife and the lack of supervision in the park. He also helped pass a law in 1883 that allowed the army to patrol Yellowstone whenever necessary.

Sheridan realized that Yellowstone needed to incorporate more land. A bill was introduced in 1883 to enlarge the park, but the railroad lobby blocked it for ten years. The railroad companies wanted to build a line up the Lamar Valley in order to control every aspect of tourism. The railroads later pushed for a water power project on the falls of the Yellowstone River. A bill was even introduced in 1892 to abolish the park itself! However, avid defenders of the national park, such as Theodore Roosevelt, were able to have the railroad bill killed.

A committee of congressmen toured the park in 1885 to assess its management. They found poachers

## THE NEZ PERCÉ WAR

The Nez Percé people were a peaceful group of Native Americans who had lived in the Wallowa Valley of eastern Oregon for many years. They had always befriended white settlers, even while defending their rights to ancestral lands. On his deathbed, old Chief Joseph made his son Joseph promise never to give up the land. In May 1877, the federal government ordered Chief Joseph (left) and his people to leave their lands in one month. Joseph would have cooperated to spare his people, but he was unable to control several trigger-happy warriors. Four whites were killed, and Joseph was forced to defend and protect his people. Leaving the Wallowa Valley, he led his band on a 1,300-mile (2,090-km) journey that took them through Yellowstone National Park.

John Shively, an old prospector, was camped on the Firehole River when Joseph's warriors captured him and forced him to be a guide. Wanting to live, Shively complied for several weeks until his escape. The day Shively was captured, several Nez Percé scouts also discovered a group of nine tourists from Radersburg, Montana. The Nez Percé forced this group, known as the Cowan party, to join them as they traveled across the Central Plateau toward Hayden Valley. When two of the tourists escaped, angry Nez Percé shot George Cowan in the head and leg and left him to die. Somehow Cowan managed to drag himself toward his original camp, only to be shot in the hip by another of Joseph's men. He was eventually rescued with a bullet protruding from his forehead. He later remarked that the army doctors were more interested in watching geysers than in treating him. The saga finally ended on October 4, 1877, just 40 miles (64 km) south of Canada near Bear Paw Mountain.

Young Chief Joseph thought he had crossed the border into Canada where his people would be safe. He was mistaken. After six days of fighting, he surrendered to federal troops, saying: "... I am tired; my heart is sick and sad. From where the sun now stands, I will fight no more forever." Chief Joseph and 431 of his people surrendered. Another 330 escaped into Canada. The Nez Percé people were sent to a reservation in Oklahoma, which was unfamiliar country for mountain people.

The north entrance gate to Yellowstone at Gardiner, Montana, dedicated by Teddy Roosevelt, used to be the main entrance to the park. Today, the other four entrances carry most of the traffic.

selling game at hotels with no fear of being punished. Their report led to the army taking over management of the park in 1886. Soldiers patrolled geyser basins. Poachers were told to stop their illegal hunting. Illegal squatters were ordered to leave, and tourist accommodations were improved. During the army's administration, an engineer named Hiram Chittenden designed wagon roads that later became the famous Grand Loop Highway used by most tourists today.

In 1894, the army was given more authority to punish poachers and hunters. It also embarked on a series of wildlife management plans to help certain animals thrive. However, as we'll see in Chapter 4, many other animals were slaughtered.

By 1907, the expansion of railroad lines brought up to 25,000 visitors to Yellowstone each year. Many wanted to know more about the science behind the park's natural phenomena. Clearly, it was time to provide guides and rangers to interpret the unique features of this wonderland.

On August 25, 1916, President Woodrow Wilson created the National Park Service, ending the army's tenure. With the arrival of the first car in 1915, the annual tourist count mushroomed as the new agency was charged "to conserve the scenery and the natural and historic objects and the wildlife therein, and to provide for the enjoyment of the same in such a manner and by such means as will leave them unimpaired for future generations." Old soldiers and scouts became park rangers—ready and able to promote and protect the park. The national park idea had survived, but there were still many lessons to learn.

Building roads in Yellowstone was often a very difficult task. These men are working on the road through the Golden Gate region.

## Chapter Three

# Thermal Wonders

*"Each geyser and each spring differs from the other in its class, style, beauty, and power. To describe them all would be an impossibility without spending weeks here...."*

— Gen. William E. Strong while viewing the Upper Geyser Basin, 1875

In Yellowstone, hot molten rock still lies close to a surface full of cracks left behind from volcanic eruptions and continual earthquakes. Water from snow and rain seeps through these openings into underground cracks. Much of the water travels down a mile or two where super-hot rock, heated by the magma sea below, raises the water's temperature. The intense combination of water, heat, and pressure results in the thermal wonders of Yellowstone—spurting geysers, bubbling hot springs, mud pots, and steaming heat vents called fumaroles.

Each thermal phenomenon looks different, but each provides the same "service." They simply release the heat that is surging upward. In Yellowstone, enough heat is released through thermal activity to melt 14 tons of ice in just one second, making it a true hot spot!

Modern geyser activity draws as much attention now as it did years ago. As many as 25,000 people gather together on a summer day to watch Old Faithful erupt. Between 200 and 250 active geysers, 60 percent of the world's total, are found in

Yellowstone, along with 10,000 other thermal features. The only other thermal region in the world like Yellowstone is Krontoski Biological Reserve located in Siberia, Russia—too far away for most people to visit.

Yellowstone's thermal regions create unique "island" environments. In winter, the ground stays warm. Sagebrush lizards—holdovers of an earlier, warmer Yellowstone—scurry along the warm, steamy surface of Norris Geyser Basin as if it were a southwestern desert. Elk and bison spend the cold months close to thermal areas. The Firehole River, fed by numerous hot springs, provides a winter hot tub and an ice-free travel route for non-migrating animals.

Yellow monkey flowers grow almost flat to the surface in late winter to early spring; in summer, they grow tall, no longer needing protection from the cold. Ross's bent grass, found only in this park, blooms in the geyser basins near Old Faithful before the snow has melted anywhere else. Other flowers blossom a month or so earlier in the spring.

Geysers erupt, hot springs bubble, mud pots gurgle, and steam vents puff. Life goes on as usual in Yellowstone's thermal basins. But to humans, these thermal features seem extraordinary.

Monkey flowers bloom in a thermal area at Madison Junction.

## Geysers Galore

The word *geyser*, meaning "gusher" or "spouter," comes from the name of Iceland's Grand Geysir. Its first eruption was recorded in 1294. Icelanders were so proud of this unique phenomenon that they copyrighted the name *geysir* so no one else could use it!

Yellowstone's geysers are located in nine geyser basins. However, the word *basin* is not an accurate description of these areas. Basins usually are bowl-shaped depressions in the ground, while Yellowstone's geyser basins are geographical regions or fields in which thermal phenomena occur. Geysers generally occur near the center of these areas, while mud pots are found on the outer fringes.

The total land area enclosed in these basins is actually very small. Upper Geyser Basin, the largest and most important geyser region in the world, is only about 0.5 miles (0.8 km) wide and 2 miles (3.2 km) long. In that small space are 180 geysers—one-fourth of the world's total. Not all of them are superstars like Old Faithful, Riverside, or

A lone elk moves past an erupting Old Faithful Geyser, hardly noticing the event.

Grand. Tiny Sponge Geyser, the park's smallest spouter, erupts every minute, shooting water up nine inches (22.8 cm). But whether geysers are big or small, they all operate on the same principles.

Geysers are rare creations—they occur only under certain specific conditions. The first and most crucial requirement is an abundant water supply. The Yellowstone Plateau receives as much as 12 feet (3.6 m) of snow in winter and additional rain in the summer. Much of the water runs off into waterways, but there is more than enough left to seep far below the surface. Second, geysers occur only in volcanic regions. Yellowstone is located in a volcanic region. Third, there has to be an underground heat source, which in Yellowstone is the superheated ocean of underground magma. Finally, the underground cracks and conduits through the porous volcanic rock must be pressure-tight, allowing no water or steam to escape. Yellowstone has huge quantities of silica-rich rhyolite. As the water travels downward, it dissolves the silica, creating a substance called sinter that lines the tubes of the geyser's plumbing system. Sinter prevents the water and steam from escaping anywhere but through the geyser's opening on the surface.

There are two kinds of geysers—cone and fountain. Cone geysers, such as Old Faithful, erupt with a steady, continuous flow through a small opening in a mound of geyserite. Geyserite is a mineral deposited when silica-rich water from below comes to the surface. Sometimes this hard but delicate mineral builds cones above the ground. It also whitewashes the ground and coats nearby tree trunks. Not all such deposits are shaped like cones, however. Castle Geyser's cone looks more like the ruins of an old castle, while Grotto Geyser's cone is a twisted formation of geyserite-smothered logs.

Fountain geysers have no cone aboveground. Instead, they erupt from a vent at the floor of a hot spring crater or from a funnel-shaped opening in the ground. Before an eruption, the water level in the hot spring rises and overflows. A great burst of

Clouds of steam rise above Midway Geyser Basin near Firehole River.

Grotto Geyser's cone is made of sinter-covered trees.

water, spreading up like a fan opening, shoots from the pool during an eruption. Unlike a cone geyser, which erupts in one continuous burst of water, fountain geysers erupt intermittently, falling and shooting up again during a single eruption. Great Fountain Geyser has a vent 16 feet (4.9 m) wide that is filled with boiling water when it is not erupting.

The timing and length of geyser eruptions vary. Most of Yellowstone's geysers erupt at irregular

## HOW A GEYSER WORKS

A geyser is a spring that shoots up hot water with great force. Geysers are formed far below the Earth's surface, where water seeps down through deep channels or tubes. The underground plumbing system of a geyser bends and twists so much that hot water cannot escape easily. The geyser tube is lined with sinter, which makes the tube pressure-tight, allowing no water or steam to get out except at the surface.

As water sinks deeper and deeper underground in the geyser tube, pressure at the bottom increases, causing the boiling point to rise. The water may be as hot as 300°F (149°C), but it can't boil and turn to steam, because pressure from the water above is too high. The water just keeps getting hotter and hotter.

Some of the water in the tube rises because it is lighter than water below. The pressure of the upper water lessens, until it reaches the boiling point. The first few boiling bubbles move up the tube, lifting the water above. Small amounts of water gurgle out of the geyser opening until enough water has been thrown out to lower the pressure farther down the geyser tube. Once pressure is lessened above, a full-scale eruption is triggered. Through a process called flashing, the superheated water below suddenly becomes steam, and a type of "chain reaction" occurs. The steam lifts more water, and the pressure is lowered, which in turn generates more steam, and the process is repeated until a rapid explosion of water and steam shoots through the opening at the surface.

The length of a geyser eruption depends on how much water has accumulated below the ground, how hot it is, and how fast it can travel through the tube. After an eruption, some of the water runs off into rivers and streams, but much of it falls back down the geyser opening or seeps through the porous rock into the geyser plumbing system again. When conditions are right, another eruption occurs. Any change in the underground fractures and passageways can change the inter-

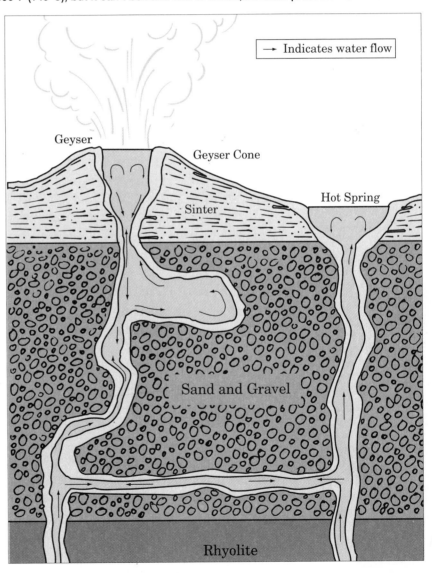

val between geyser eruptions. Scientists have also found that the plumbing systems among some of the geyser regions are connected so that a change in one basin may affect thermal activity in another.

Echinus Geyser erupts every 35 to 75 minutes, with eruptions lasting from 6 minutes to more than an hour. Its water is as acidic as vinegar—a very rare occurrence. Most of the world's acid-water geysers are located in Yellowstone's Norris Geyser Basin.

intervals, but some are remarkably predictable. Old Faithful has shot 3,700 to 8,400 gallons (14,006 to 31,795 l) of water skyward 100 to 185 feet (30 to 56 m) every 35 to 95 minutes since it was first observed by the Hayden expedition. The length of an eruption is usually about 2 to 5 minutes.

Other geysers erupt more regularly. Echinus Geyser in Norris Geyser Basin is a favorite because you can get closer to it than to any other large geyser, and the average interval between eruptions is 20 to 80 minutes. Echinus is a fountain geyser with eruptions lasting anywhere from a few minutes to more than an hour.

On the other hand, you might have to wait years to see an eruption of Steamboat Geyser, the world's largest and most powerful geyser. First observed in 1878, the geyser has erupted to a height of 400 feet (122 m), releasing over a million gallons (3,785,412 l) of water. The water phase lasts from 5 to 20 minutes, but steam sometimes roars from the opening for several hours. These powerful eruptions have been heard as far as 14 miles (22.5 km) away in Madison Junction, Wyoming. The last major eruption occurred on October 4, 1991.

Geologists don't really know what makes one geyser erupt regularly and another irregularly. They do know, however, that almost all thermal features are interconnected through an underground plumbing system. One group of geysers and hot springs might become less active as the activity of another group increases. For example, Daisy Geyser was a regularly active geyser in the Upper Geyser Basin, while neighboring Bonita Hot Pool was fairly calm. Somehow that changed in the early 1960s when Bonita began to overflow and erupt as a geyser. Over the next 13 years, Daisy erupted only three times. In the 1970s, Daisy's eruptions again became very regular and predictable. Bonita is now almost completely still. Scientists think earthquakes might have caused a shift in the underground plumbing tubes.

The Fountain Hotel used to stand on a hill next to Thud Geyser, in the Lower Geyser Basin. Before the hotel burned to the ground in 1927, employees and visitors used the geyser crater as a giant trash can. In 1948, park rangers tried to clean the geyser, hoping it would become more active. They recovered numerous articles from the 15- by 18-foot (4.6- by 5.5-m) crater. Some of the stranger objects included two Colorado tax tokens, bones, a 40-gallon (151-l) drum, a bath towel, a bath mat, a raincoat, one horseshoe, a pitchfork, two drawer handles, two cake molds, a 1913 Yellowstone guidebook, one lightbulb, two ear tags for Idaho cattle, an oven rack, a cotton coat, and a petroleum jelly jar. Unfortunately, the cleaning didn't help—Thud is no longer active.

# Hot Springs and Pools

Unlike geysers, the underground plumbing of a hot spring or pool is fairly straight and unrestricted, so water isn't trapped beneath the surface. Depending on the heat below, some springs are calm, while others boil vigorously and overflow. These striking thermal features come in every color of the rainbow.

The largest and probably the most colorful pool in Yellowstone is Grand Prismatic. Located in Midway Geyser Basin near Firehole River, it measures 370 feet (113 m) across and pours gallons of hot water into the river. Sometimes it is difficult to see the full majesty of this spring because huge clouds of steam hang over its surface. These steam clouds often reflect the green, red, yellow, and blue of the water below, giving the pool an unearthly appearance.

Some hot springs, such as Shell Spring in Upper Geyser Basin, churn and boil continuously (above). Others, such as Grand Pristmatic Spring (left), are more calm. Grand Prismatic is one of the largest hot springs in the world.

Algae growing in Grand Prismatic Spring adds a splash of bright color.

There is nothing quite as spectacular as Mammoth Hot Springs. Unusual travertine terraces that one traveler called "caves turned inside out" cover Terrace Mountain. Travertine is the name given to calcium carbonate when it has been deposited aboveground. As hot water moves to the surface through a maze of underground cracks and channels, it passes through limestone. The lime is dissolved with the aid of carbon dioxide, forming calcium carbonate. As the water oozes out at ground level through small openings, little pools of water collect. The calcium carbonate is deposited faster on the outer part of these pools, producing a travertine lip that holds the rest of the water in. Eventually

Mammoth Hot Springs
is made up of springs,
mounds, and terraces
covering Terrace
Mountain near park
headquarters.

Mammoth Hot Springs
is famous for its colorful
travertine terraces.

these pools fill up and overflow, forming other pools, which build other terraces.

Travertine terraces cover the entire hillside like giant marshmallow steps. Much of the travertine is over 150 feet (46 m) thick. These formations are constantly changing as vents are blocked, and water flows to new places. The terraces left behind dry to a stark white and ultimately become gray and brittle. Some contain algae that tint the white with pastel colors.

Color is the one universal characteristic of hot springs. Some of the deep blue pools simply reflect the blue of the sky. Other colors come from suspended or dissolved minerals in the water. Sulfur makes a bright yellow color—as well as the rotten egg smell that causes many visitors to hold their noses. Arsenic sulfides create bright oranges and yellows, iron oxides produce browns and reds, and iron pyrites make black and gray.

These mineral pools, with their bright colors and unpleasant odors, inspired early explorers to give them "devilish" names, as if they were parts of hell. On the banks of Yellowstone River, Sulfur

Cauldron's churning yellow waters are acidic enough to destroy clothing. Seething Black Dragon's Cauldron near Mud Volcano looks like boiling black tar sloshing from a steamy vent. And tiny black balls of iron bob on the boiling white waters of Cinder Pool.

Another source of color in the spring is living things. Bacteria and tiny plants called algae have adapted to thrive on the rocky surfaces of the hot springs, creating a huge palette of beautiful colors. One microbiologist commented, "Yellowstone is like going to heaven. This is where you can see how bacteria and blue-green algae adapt to various properties of the hot springs and pools. This must be like the way things were a billion and a half or two billion years ago, before some of the higher forms of life evolved."

Some bacteria do not depend on the sun for energy. Instead, they use sulfur and methane for their energy source in a process called chemosynthesis. At Evening Primrose Spring a bacteria called *Sulfolobus acidocaldarius* uses sulfur to produce sulfuric acid. The chemical reaction makes a layer of bright yellow foam on the surface, acidic enough to dissolve clothing.

The lightest-colored plants live in the hottest water, and the darkest-colored plants in cooler water. Bright yellow plants thrive in water that is about 160°F (71°C), orange plants thrive at 145°F (63°C), brown plants at 130°F (54°C), and green plants at 120°F (49°C). Some pink and pale yellow bacteria can survive at 180°F (82°C). Mixtures of algae can produce such hues as fluorescent chartreuse. Runoff streams from hot springs often look like a rippling rainbow, since water close to the center is warmer than that on the edges.

*Fishing Cone is one of Yellowstone's most famous hot springs. Supposedly, a fisherman could catch a fish in the lake and cook it in this boiling spring without even removing the fish from the hook! Today, however, Fishing Cone is no longer hot enough to cook fish. Because water levels have changed over the years, Fishing Cone is usually covered by cold water unless the lake is very low.*

**Morning Glory Pool in Upper Geyser Basin was named after the morning glory flower. Debris thrown into the pool has caused the temperature to drop. The pool's color is changing as brown and green algae spread toward the center.**

**Black Dragon's Cauldron (below) near Mud Volcano is a muddy hot spring, known for its smell and not its beauty. It exploded into existence in 1948.**

# Mud Pots and Fumaroles

Mud pots are hot springs that are in the process of becoming blocked with mud. They are often found on the outer fringes of geyser basins where there isn't as much water, but they also occur throughout the park. Sulfuric acid breaks down subterranean rock to produce fine-grained mud. Gas and steam trapped in this thick mush make the mixture gurgle, plop, and bubble. The rotten-egg smell of hydrogen sulfide hangs over these areas.

When water is scarce, mud pots look like thick oatmeal. Sometimes huge blobs of grayish-brown clay are thrown out, covering the surrounding ground and trees with a muddy frosting. When water is more plentiful, the same mud pots may be as runny as soup. Then, thanks to dissolved minerals, they have all the lovely color of a spring garden—soft pinks, orange, and blue.

Mud pots come in all sizes. When Mud Volcano, one of the largest, was discovered by the Washburn expedition in 1870, its 35-foot (11-m) walls surrounded a 30-foot- (9-m-) wide crater of churning gray clay. Without warning, big chunks of mud were thrown from the crater, covering the ground and surrounding lodgepole pines like an electric mixer gone wild. Mud Volcano is still thought to be moody and evil-looking, but it is no longer as active.

Throughout the park, fumaroles, or steam vents, huff and puff. These openings allow superheated steam to escape from far below the Earth's

Scientists believe that one of Yellowstone's major lava vents is located near Mud Volcano. The smell of "rotten eggs" is strong, as hydrogen sulfide gas from deep below the surface escapes. The grayish color of the mud is caused by sulfur in the form of iron sulfide.

Fumeroles change with the seasons. When rain and snow are plentiful, they become boiling mud pots. In July and August, the "mud" becomes thicker. By late summer, only steam escapes from cracked mud at Grizzly Fumerole near Mud Volcano.

Roaring Mountain is covered with steam vents so powerful that trees have been killed by the escaping gases.

surface, often baking the ground. On Roaring Mountain, small but powerful vents near the summit have released enough hydrogen sulfide and heat over a period of years to kill the trees on the hillside. Roaring Mountain is not as active today, so new seedlings have had a chance to grow.

## The Future of the Hot Spot

Yellowstone's unique thermal features have always attracted attention. After a trip through Yellowstone between 1838 and 1839, Osborne Russell wrote: "What a field of speculation this presents for chemist and geologist…." The same fascination remains today. These unpredictable, fragile, and sometimes deadly phenomena are always changing.

Natural forces such as earthquakes continue to affect the thermal basins. In October 1983, an earthquake 200 miles (322 km) away from Yellowstone near Borah Peak in Idaho caused Old Faithful to slow down. Other geysers, however, increased in activity.

Natural forces cannot be stopped. But destructive human activity can upset the balance of nature. Conservationists are worried that drilling for oil, gas, or hot water outside park boundaries could disturb the delicate underwater plumbing system. A tiny leak could undermine an entire geyser field. Whenever humans have tried to harness the energy from thermal regions, geysers have been affected. Iceland's geysers have diminished, New Zealand's great thermal fields are gone, and Chile's are now also dying. Energy development has changed the underground openings so water and heat no longer flow as they once did. With careful planning, the United States will be able to protect Yellowstone's thermal regions from a similar fate.

The lava vents near Old Faithful and in the Mud Volcano area (below) are still active today. They are called "resurging domes." Scientists are watching these areas closely for any signs of new volcanic activity.

## THE GEYSER BASINS OF YELLOWSTONE

Upper Geyser Basin, located farther upstream on Firehole River than Midway or Lower Geyser basins, is the most important thermal region in the world. It is the home of such well-known geysers as Old Faithful, Beehive, Grand, and Riverside. Castle Geyser (opposite page) has one of the three largest cones in Yellowstone. Hundreds of beautiful hot springs and geysers are found here.

Midway Geyser Basin covers a 1-mile- (1.6-km-) long area next to Firehole River, but most of the thermal features in this small basin are large. Grand Prismatic Spring, the biggest single hot spring on Earth, and Excelsior Geyser, with a crater measuring 200 by 300 feet (61 by 91 km), are located here.

Lower Geyser Basin covers the largest area of any geyser basin, about 5 square miles (12.9 sq km). The best-known geysers include Great Fountain (bottom), Fountain, Clepsydra, and White Dome, which has one of the three largest cones in the park. Fountain Paint Pots also are located here.

Norris Geyser Basin (top) is different from the other basins in several ways. Its waters are very acidic, since large amounts of sulfur are brought to the surface. It is also the hottest basin. A strange annual occurrence, known as the "disturbance," takes place in Norris Geyser Basin in August or September. Within several hours, hot springs and geysers become muddy, quiet springs erupt, and geysers become more active. But no one knows why. Echinus Geyser, Steamboat Geyser, and Porcelain Basin are other famous attractions in this region.

Most of the thermal activity in West Thumb Geyser Basin occurs in a region less than 1,000 feet (305 m) in length. Located on the shore of Yellowstone Lake, it is known for its hot pools. No more than six geysers have been seen here. West Thumb Geyser Basin is home to the Abyss and Black pools, Fishing Cone Hot Spring, and Thumb Paint Pots.

Measuring 1,600 feet by 800 feet (488 m to 244 m), Shoshone Geyser Basin is one of the most important thermal regions in the world, though it is rarely visited. This region probably contains 70 geysers, including Minute Man Geyser, first described by trapper Osborne Russell in 1839. During the early years of the park, this basin was visited by tourists as often as any other thermal region, but today it can be reached only by hikers. No detailed maps were made of Shoshone Geyser Basin until the late 1960s.

The Artists' Paint Pots attract visitors to Gibbon Geyser Basin. The vivid colors of these mud pots, along with the beautiful hot springs and bright green forests, make this region one of the most colorful spots in Yellowstone.

Lone Star Geyser Basin lies 5 miles (8 km) up Firehole River from Old Faithful. The basin was named for Lone Star Geyser. Its cone is over 9 feet (2.7 m) tall, making it one of the three largest in Yellowstone.

Heart Lake Geyser Basin (above right) is the least visited of the major geyser basins in the park. Hikers sometimes feel that they are the first people to ever enter the region when they see it for the first time.

# Chapter Four

# Life in Wildness

Elk near Mammoth Hot Springs raise their heads, twisting their ears forward to listen. They detect even the slightest movement. The elk have been eating grass and herbs on the summer range. Some of them will leave to spend the winter season in the national forests outside the boundaries of the park.

Far away in the craggy mountains, a tiny pika—a relative of the rabbit—also gets ready for winter. When elk and coyotes move to the lower valleys, and bighorn sheep go where there is less snow cover, the tiny pika continues to live in piles of broken rock at or near the timberline. During August and September, this 6-inch (15.2-cm) creature scurries around gathering grass, stems, and flowers to dry in "haystacks." The food is stored under rocks for the long winter ahead.

Everywhere in the wildness of Yellowstone, living things interact. Any change in any part of any habitat has consequences. When Yellowstone became a park in 1872, it was to be a place for the preservation of life. But these words meant something entirely different then. Bear, elk, bison, fish, and other plant and animal species were tampered with, often with disastrous results.

## Plentiful Plants

Yellowstone National Park is home to 1,700 plant species, but one stands out because of its sheer numbers. Only 13 kinds of trees grow here, covering 80 percent of the park with forests. Sixty percent of those forests are dense stands of lodgepole pine. The tree looks unusual because its lower tree branches fall off, leaving a bare trunk up to 75 feet (23 m) tall. At the top of these toothpick trunks, the remaining green branches look like small trees perched high above the ground. Native Americans used lodgepole tree trunks to build the frames for their tepees.

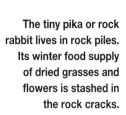

The tiny pika or rock rabbit lives in rock piles. Its winter food supply of dried grasses and flowers is stashed in the rock cracks.

"In Yellowstone, the resource is not 20,000 elk, or a million lodgepole pines, or a grizzly bear. The resource is wildness. The interplay of all the parts of the wilderness...acting upon each other to create the wild setting, creates a state of existence, a wildness, that is the product and the resource for which Yellowstone is being preserved."

—Don Despain, Yellowstone plant ecologist as quoted in *Playing God in Yellowstone*, 1984

Lodgepole pine trees grow in poor rhyolitic soil at elevations from 7,600 to about 9,000 feet (2,316 to about 2,743 m). Trees living in poor soil at such high altitudes grow very slowly. A 300-year-old tree may have a trunk measuring only 3 to 4 inches (7.6 to 10.1 cm) in diameter. Since their roots cannot grow deep, many of the pines topple over and litter the forest floor.

Dense lodgepole pine forests cover Yellowstone near Shoshone Lake. The Grand Tetons can be seen in the distance.

Because the trees grow close together and the soil is poor, only a few shrubs and herbs can grow in the ground below. Lodgepole forests are called "biological deserts," since they lack a diversity of plant and animal life. Moose, elk, or deer wander through looking for food, and a few small mammals and birds call these forests home. Only natural phenomena such as forest fires and insect plagues can renew these old forests. New plants gain a foothold before the trees recover or grow back.

Because aspen trees grow at Yellowstone's lower elevations that most people visit, they seem more plentiful than they actually are. Aspen make up about 2 percent of the plant growth in the northern regions of Yellowstone.

Engelmann spruce, subalpine fir, and whitebark pine trees usually grow at higher elevations. Few people see these forests because they grow above 8,400 feet (2,560 m). One small bird—the Clark's nutcracker—plays a part in spreading the seeds of whitebark pine into lodgepole forests and into meadows and fields. Toward the end of summer, this busy bird gathers large quantities of pine nuts in its mouth and hides them. Botanists think the nutcracker must forget many of its hiding places. The unused stashes sprout as tiny whitebark pines.

Treeless habitats are especially important in Yellowstone. Large meadows, such as Gibbon

# INSECTS AND TREES

Mountain pine bark beetles infest old pine trees with trunk diameters over 8 inches (20.3 cm). Female beetles bore into the inner bark and lay eggs. They also deposit a tree-weakening fungus. After the larvae hatch, they cut off the tree's nutrients by eating the inner bark. The needles on the pine turn orange as the tree begins to die. It takes about 10 to 15 years for the older trees to die, opening the forest floor to sunlight for new plant growth. This is nature's way of thinning the pines and providing more food for animals such as deer and elk.

During the 1930s, 4,000 insect-infested pine trees growing on Mount Washburn's slopes were cut down to stop the pest. It didn't work. The pine beetles simply attacked the trees left standing, destroying the entire forest. Today, beetles and other insects, such as the western spruce budworm, are allowed to infest the forests of lodgepole pine, Engelmann spruce, and subalpine fir as part of the natural tree-thinning cycle. DDT is no longer sprayed from planes to kill the budworm as it was in the 1950s. That dangerous chemical not only killed insects, but it also was detected in fish over 80 miles (129 km) away. The park service has learned that insects are an important part of the natural cycle.

Meadow, Pelican Valley, and Hayden Valley, are all that is left of ancient lake bottoms. Sedges, wheatgrass, oatgrass, shrubs such as cinquefoil, and small willows grow in the fine glacial soil. Bison use the wet sedge meadows in the Lamar Valley for their food supply. Other open areas, such as the dry grasslands near Mammoth and Gardiner, Montana, are drier, receiving only about 11 inches (27.9 cm) of rain a year. These areas have green grasses in the spring but dry out by summer. Grasses are interspersed with such plants as sagebrush and rabbitbrush. Sagebrush has adapted so that it produces large leaves when there is moisture and smaller ones when water is scarce. The drier, open areas add to the winter diet of elk and bighorn sheep.

Pronghorn antelope feed in Yellowstone's plains and grasslands during the summer.

## Patterns of Life

In all ecosystems, including Yellowstone, there are numerous relationships between plants and animals. Over 40 percent of the mammals in Yellowstone are plant-eating rodents, such as gophers, squirrels, chipmunks, and mice. Animals that eat mostly plants are called herbivores. Large, hoofed animals called ungulates, such as bison, elk, moose, pronghorn antelope, and bighorn sheep, also eat plants. These herbivores are primary prey for carnivores, or meat-eating animals, such as coyotes, mountain lions, and bears whose appetite for meat may keep some animal populations in check. Carnivores can also sometimes be scavengers, eating animals killed during winter, or by disease, starvation, or other animals. Another group, called omnivores, eat whatever plant or animal food they can find. As long as these patterns are not disturbed, all is well.

In Yellowstone, well-intentioned people who considered natural predators to be "bad" animals interrupted these patterns. Coyotes, mountain lions, bobcats, and gray wolves attacked Yellowstone's "good" animals. These were the ungulates, such as the elk, moose, and bison, that attracted tourists and money to the park. Naturally, most people thought these animals needed some protection. Systematic predator extermination began shortly after the park was created. The size of an early park ranger's paycheck depended on how many wolf pelts he turned in. As late as 1932, Park Superintendent Toll said: "We have always assumed that elk and the deer and the antelope were the type of animals the park was for.... To me a herd of antelope and deer is more valuable than a herd of coyotes." The predator extermination continued until the 1940s.

Managing the population of "good" animals began right after the park was created. When it was discovered in 1902 that approximately 25 bison remained, saving these animals became a national cause. Bison bulls were brought in from Texas. These animals were bred with bison from Montana and with some of the remaining Yellowstone bison. Land in the Slough Creek Valley and Lamar Valley was plowed and planted with timothy grass and oats. A "buffalo" ranch was created within the park where crossbred animals were fed. These animals were kept in corrals during the night and let out during the day. By 1915, the bison from "Buffalo Ranch" were allowed to roam free. Winter feeding programs were phased out by 1950.

Bison calves are born in May or June. During the summer, bison herds graze in the Hayden Valley, on the Madison and Mirror plateaus, and in the Lamar Valley.

Bison in Yellowstone now number about 4,000. Winter is a significant bison predator, but wolves, a natural predator, have been exterminated. Dead and dying bison provide food for grizzlies, but the easygoing bear doesn't usually exert energy to chase healthy bison.

Because of harsh Yellowstone winters, many bison migrate out of the park, where they cannot be protected, looking for food. The bison in the picture is foraging near Old Faithful Geyser.

With their population so high, some bison are forced to look for range outside the park. Ranchers become particularly anxious when bison leave the park because they carry brucellosis, an organism that can cause pregnant cattle to abort their young. Although there has never been a documented case of this organism being transferred to cattle, bison straying outside park boundaries have been legally killed for decades to protect livestock. Management of bison that migrate outside the park is still a source of contention. Since the park supports a policy of natural management of animals, their movement outside the park is not discouraged. However, the federal government has no control once animals leave the park.

## Animal Superstars

As fall approaches, elk move to the Gallatin River Valley, Swan Lake Flats, and other lower elevations for the September mating ritual called rutting. The goal of a male elk is to claim as many female cows as possible—his harem may number up to 20.

By November, mating is completed, and the elk begin to migrate to winter ranges. The Madison-Firehole herd stays within the park near thermal regions. The largest Yellowstone herd, numbering 20,800, winters in northern Yellowstone and outside the park's boundaries along the Yellowstone River. In May, the herds begin migrating back into the park and their summer feeding ranges, and the cycle begins anew.

When the bison population was threatened in the 1800s, the army thought elk also were in trouble. Feeding programs, started before 1900,

## ADOLPH MURIE AND COYOTES

During the 1930s, a study by biologist Adolph Murie resulted in a book entitled *Ecology of the Coyote in Yellowstone.* Murie helped debunk the myth that predators were "bad" animals that preyed on "innocent" ungulates. He showed that most coyotes are simply good scavengers. They feed on deer that have died from malnutrition, parasites, or disease. Murie found no evidence to support the notion that coyotes track down and hunt healthy deer. Instead, he discovered that deer often chase coyotes! He reported that the survival of deer depended on a good supply of sagebrush and young herbs—the same food sources used by other ungulates whose populations had increased because predators were killed.

Elk calves are born in late spring, as the elk herds return to Yellowstone for the summer months.

continued for years as predators were exterminated. When fences, towns, and other developments sprang up, many migration routes to winter ranges were cut off.

During the particularly harsh winters of 1909, 1910, and 1911, thousands of elk starved south of the park near Jackson Hole, Wyoming. Those that survived were in terrible condition. Alarmed by so much death, the federal government established the National Elk Refuge in 1912 as a winter range.

But by the 1930s, park biologists decided the elk population was too big. They began blaming these animals for a host of problems, including habitat degradation.

Rangers then began to control elk populations by shooting, trapping, or moving animals to various locations. However, as biologists learned more about elk, park management began to take a different approach. A program that encouraged natural management of elk populations and restored winter ranges outside the park began. For example, the Rocky Mountain Elk Foundation in Missoula, Montana, bought over 9,000 acres (3,642 ha) of elk winter range north of the park in cooperation with the National Park Service. The land was sold to the forest service in 1993, preserving habitat in Gallatin National Forest for migrating elk.

Although elk populations are very large, most people first think of bears when they think of

Courtship starts when the male elk begins bugling. This loud, low guttural sound rises to a very high pitch and tapers off to low grunts. Frequent and intense bugling warns rivals to stay away. But males often challenge each other anyway, locking antlers and sparring until one gives up.

# THE RETURN OF THE WOLF

The wolf has been one of the most hated and misunderstood animals on Earth. By 1877, gray wolves were poisoned in Yellowstone for their hides. Later, as settlers came to the region surrounding the park, federal agents continued the extermination. Soon there were no more wolves in Yellowstone.

Valuable predators, wolves hunt elk, deer, bison, and mule deer, killing the vulnerable and weak. Since the mid-1980s, park rangers have been calling for the reintroduction of the wolf. They believe several packs of wolves— or about 100 animals—could easily live in the park. Most Americans agree with the rangers, but local ranchers don't. They think wolves will kill their livestock, even though the rangers plan to control wolves that cause problems outside the park boundaries and compensate ranchers for livestock losses. Although plans to return wolves have been delayed because of the ranchers' protests, the animals might be coming back to Yellowstone on their own. A few wolves have already migrated from Canada to Glacier National Park in northwestern Montana. Some scientists believe it may be only a few years before gray wolves move south to their ancestral home in Yellowstone.

Yellowstone. The combined population of the two species in Yellowstone—black bears and grizzly bears—is at least 900.

Black bears are actually black, brown, or cinnamon. It is hard to imagine that these animals weigh less than 1 pound (0.4 kg) at birth because adults are so large, weighing up to 350 pounds (159 kg). Black bears used to roam along the park's roads and beg visitors for food. Today, they prefer the privacy of forested habitats. Their powerful curved claws allow them to climb trees in search of food or to get away from their more powerful cousins, grizzly bears.

The grizzly bear is one of the largest carnivores on Earth, weighing up to 600 pounds (272 kg). Its fur ranges from light brown to black with silver-tipped hairs. Unlike the black bear, the grizzly has a distinctive hump between its shoulders. Everything about this animal indicates power, from its shuffling walk to its deadly 4-inch (10-cm) straight claws. Unlike black bears, grizzlies cannot climb trees.

When grizzly bears come out of their dens in April, they spend most of their time eating. Since they are omnivores, they consume just about anything that is easy to get. Covering up to 300 square miles (777 sq km) in one "eating" season, they can consume up to 40,000 calories a day during the late summer and fall. This tremendous appetite prepares them for their seven-month winter nap. Bears eat elk, cutthroat trout, and plants such as dandelions, clover, thistle, and berries. Army cutworm moths scooped from high mountain slopes are a prized delicacy. In fall, the grizzly moves to high

**The black bear has a straight back, a straight facial profile, and curved claws.**

**Black bears are common in Yellowstone, with a population of about 650 animals. Black bears like to stay in forested areas.**

country where the red squirrel has stashed white bark pine nuts. These fat-laden nuts give the bear its last feast before winter.

Perhaps no other animal has been manipulated more than the grizzly bear. Since 1902, park rules have prohibited feeding bears. Grizzlies were once allowed to eat at open dumps, however, while visitors watched from grandstands. Dump feeding kept these popular animals close enough to make visitors happy.

Dump feeding continued for decades. Two naturalists—Drs. John and Frank Craighead—were hired by the National Park Service in 1959 and began an 11-year grizzly bear study. As the study came to a close, the park superintendent decided to establish a policy of natural management for grizzly bears. This meant closing the dumps—a move the Craigheads argued against. They thought that grizzlies, having become accustomed to easy food, should be weaned off garbage very slowly. Otherwise, the results could be disastrous. The park superintendent believed that, although the number of bears might drop at first, the population would eventually stabilize as the bears used natural food sources.

Grizzlies weren't used to getting their food in the backcountry, however. And with all the new development and logging outside the park, the Craigheads doubted whether enough good-quality habitat remained in which the bears could find

Unlike the black bear, a grizzly bear has a shoulder hump, a curved snout, and straighter claws.

Grizzly bears inhabit meadows, although they are never too far from the cover of trees.

enough food to stay healthy. They also thought this new policy would simply push the grizzlies into closer contact with people in the campgrounds, and that the end result would be fewer grizzlies. The dumps were closed in 1970 and 1971 anyway.

The bears were then expected to return to the backcountry and live on natural food sources. In 1973, the Interagency Grizzly Bear Study Team, a group of research biologists from federal government agencies and the states of Idaho, Montana, and Wyoming, was established to study the behavior of the grizzlies after the dump closures. In 1973, they reported that the population had dropped to 200 bears. They predicted a dismal future for the bear unless deaths were kept low.

Park rangers tag grizzlies so they can follow the movements of each bear.

In addition to the garbage dump policy, another park policy can aggravate the grizzly bear problem. Bears, who often return to developed areas of the park in search of food, are removed. If they return too many times, they are killed or taken to zoos by park rangers.

Some believe the closure of the dumps in Yellowstone caused the decline in the bear population. But promoters of natural management say that the earlier grizzly population was not natural in behavior or numbers and that the number of bears was artificially high. Others say that climatic conditions may be the biggest factor of all. If it is too dry, as it was in the 1960s when the bears were still eating at dumps, there isn't enough food to fatten bears before hibernation or to feed females and their cubs.

Even though opinions are wide-ranging, all scientists agree that grizzlies are voracious eaters and need big areas to search for food. A large part of that range is outside the park where development and logging have changed the natural habitat.

Government policies continue to change as researchers learn more about grizzly behavior. For example, in the early 1980s, it was discovered that, as more visitors came to Yellowstone to fish and hike in the backcountry, the bears simply left these areas. Scientists call this "avoidance behavior." With grizzly habitat shrinking outside and inside the park, there were fewer places for the grizzlies to go to find food and live. In 1983, the park established Grizzly Bear Management Areas—regions in Yellowstone where grizzlies can roam, free of humans, during certain times of the year. This program has been very successful, and grizzlies have returned to backcountry areas.

When bears continue to come into populated areas, they are removed to backcountry areas.

Keeping bear deaths low and monitoring the number of cubs born was another goal of managers. By 1986, the number of grizzly bear cubs born was at an all-time high. Researchers are, however, still trying to determine how many bears are needed to ensure their future survival. That is very difficult, since animal populations are always changing as the climate and other factors change.

Although the grizzly seems to be doing quite well now, its long-term survival is still in question. Most conservationists hope that short-term success will not mean that the bear will no longer be listed as "threatened" by the federal government. If that happens, there would be less legal pressure on government or private landowners to preserve habitat. Some scientists think that supplementary feeding might be necessary at some point in the future to keep the bears in Yellowstone, but probably not for some time.

Although not as plentiful as elk, bighorn sheep are more easily seen in the park than bears are. Bighorn are excellent mountain climbers. They appear on what look like unreachable ledges and slopes. Their round hooves, depressed in the middle and sharp on the edges, grab the ledges like tiny suction cups. Hundreds of these majestic sheep used to comb the alpine meadows in summer, but once again, humans upset the balance. Hunting, as well as disease and parasites from sheep, has reduced the population. About 300 remain today.

Male and female bighorn sheep have horns, but female horns are much smaller and slightly curved. The males' curling horns may represent over 10 percent of his body weight. Unlike elk, the bighorn males' horns are permanent and continue growing until he dies. A male's status is determined by the size of his horns. Two males with horns of almost equal size often engage in head-butting until one gives up. This is hardly ever fatal, since the animal's skull is naturally shock-resistant.

Most Yellowstone visitors are not able to see a grizzly bear. This photographer was able to get close enough to catch the bear's facial expression.

Some visitors are lucky enough to see bighorn sheep on the rocky ledges of the Grand Canyon of the Yellowstone River or on the slopes of Mount Washburn.

Trumpeter swans have made a comeback in Yellowstone.

## Animals of the Air

Although mammals get most of the attention in Yellowstone, the park is home to 279 species of birds, including the unique trumpeter swan. Their clear, haunting call floats on the air for a long distance. Trumpeter swans stand 4 feet (1.2 m) tall, with wingspans up to 6.5 feet (2 m). These birds mate for life and may live over 20 years.

Trumpeter swans used to be more numerous than they are today, but they were killed for meat and feathers. In 1932, fewer than 100 birds remained. Yellowstone biologists found a small population in the Centennial Valley of Montana and recommended that the Red Rock Lakes area of Montana be set aside for preserving the trumpeter swan. In 1935, the Red Rock Lakes National Wildlife Refuge was established. Today approximately 400 trumpeter swans live within the Greater Yellowstone region in the summer, while the winter population can exceed 2,000.

Early park managers destroyed pelican eggs, thinking the bird was depleting the fish supply. Today, visitors are not allowed near the breeding grounds at Molly Island in Yellowstone Lake. The pelican is now thriving.

## An Uncertain Future

Today, two of Yellowstone's mammal species and two bird species are threatened or endangered. Other animals are rare or at risk. Losing any one of Yellowstone's species is a critical loss for other species and for visitors who come to see the animals in the United States' largest wildlife preserve.

It has taken wildlife managers a long time to learn that nature manages the park better than

# FISH IN YELLOWSTONE

There are over 200 lakes in Yellowstone National Park, but none is as beautiful as Yellowstone Lake. This giant lake covers 136 square miles (352 sq km), reaching a maximum depth of 390 feet (119 m). One of the early Yellowstone explorers, Ferdinand V. Hayden, wrote in 1871: "...a vast sheet of quiet water, of a most delicate ultramarine hue, one of the most beautiful scenes I have ever beheld...." Early explorers thought the shape of the lake resembled a left hand with a thumb and three fingers. The Yellowstone River is the lake's main outlet at Fishing Bridge, and over 120 tributaries empty into its waters.

The lake never gets warmer than 52°F (11°C), but it is an ideal place for the largest inland cutthroat trout population in the world. Named for the red markings below its gills, the cutthroat (right) is one of 12 native species in the park.

Cutthroat trout, usually found in waters that drain into the Pacific Ocean, migrated to the Yellowstone region through a marshy wetland over Two Ocean Pass on the Continental Divide just outside the park's southeast boundary. Today they are the dominant fish species.

When the park was established, about 40 percent of its waters had no fish. The waterfalls prevent the movement of fish up rivers and streams. In the 1880s, techniques had already been developed for fish "farming," and early park administrators were determined to fill Yellowstone's waters with fish that would bring anglers and money. In 1889, when fish stocking began, almost every waterway and lake was stocked. Different species were introduced, including brown trout from Germany, salmon and brook trout from the East, and lake trout from the Great Lakes. Later, bait fishermen unintentionally brought in other species such as shiners, chubs, and suckers. Some species, such as black bass and salmon, didn't survive; others, such as yellow perch, thrived so well they had to be poisoned. Rainbow trout and brown trout drove native cutthroat and grayling out of some areas. Tiny Isa Lake (right), which straddles the Continental Divide, was one lake, however, that has never had any fish.

The cutthroat population was also threatened in other ways. First, cutthroat eggs were sent out of the park to fish farms. By 1956, over 800 million eggs from female cutthroats had been shipped. Second, thinking that the supply of cutthroat was endless, park officials allowed Yellowstone Lake to be overfished. Fishing Bridge, located where the Yellowstone River leaves the lake, was once the most popular fishing spot in the park. In the 1960s, about 49,000 fishermen were still fishing there every year, and the trout population was diminishing. When this area was closed to fishing in 1973, the trout began to recover. Other protective regulations, such as the smaller size limit, also helped. Today, trout return to spawn at the Fishing Bridge after the ice leaves Yellowstone Lake in May or June. Millions of eggs are deposited in the gravel. Nowadays, people come simply to watch fish or to catch and release them.

humans. Every plant and animal in Yellowstone National Park, and the entire Greater Yellowstone Ecosystem, occupies an important niche, or place in the ecosystem. Managers are trying to restore the natural plant and animal cycles that were upset in the past. They are also trying to encourage natural maintenance for the future. *Audubon Magazine* writer Ted Williams stated the challenge in 1989: "Trusting nature is worth a try because trusting ourselves hasn't worked. Never have humans known enough about nature to force it to do their will."

# Chapter Five

# Fire Power

During the summer of 1988, the Yellowstone region was hit with the worst fire season in its recorded history. Over 249 fires were reported. Although the fires did no great harm to the plant and animal life of the area, they did bring change to the lives and livelihood of people—and many people do not like change. In the end, one life was lost, property was destroyed, and tourist dollars plummeted.

Unlike most humans, nature thrives on change and adapts to it very quickly. Instead of destroying the Yellowstone region, fire has rearranged and renewed Yellowstone's plant and animal communities as part of a never-ending cycle. A burned forest

can be as vital to the ecosystem as a green, mature one. Often, from the nutrient-rich ashes spring new green shoots. Charred upright trees, called snags, provide more housing for woodpeckers, squirrels, and bats. These supposedly "dead" trees may not fall over for several decades. If Yellowstone is to be preserved, we need to understand the importance of fire in maintaining its plant and animal communities.

*"This is just a moment in time and to have to wait forty or fifty years for a forest to return isn't very long when you're looking at millions of years since creation. It would be best if man just stepped back, and let Yellowstone heal itself."*

**—Terry McKim,
Chief Investigator,
United Animal Nations,
1989**

**Most of the fires in Yellowstone in 1988 were caused naturally by dry lightning.**

## To Burn or Not to Burn

The people who had lived here for thousands of years understood the connection between forests and fires, but few Europeans chose to benefit from the knowledge of Native Americans. In 1886, when the army took over administration of the park to protect the forests and wildlife, they ignored everything Native Americans knew about fire. How could frequent burning of a forested area, a meadow, or a pasture yield more succulent plants for elk, bison, and horses to eat? The army administrators

*The Blackfoot people derived their name from fire. They used it so often as a weapon and as a tool that their feet were always black from traveling through ashes.*

believed they must put out every campfire gone wild and every blaze caused by lightning.

Fire suppression continued for years. Like predator extermination, putting out every fire seemed like a "good" way to protect "good" forests. Public attitudes were further reinforced by Walt Disney's classic film *Bambi* and Smokey the Bear's warning finger and thoughtful words, "Remember, only you can prevent forest fires."

However, as public attitudes called for fire suppression, scientists were rediscovering the truth. Fire was not a careless destroyer—it was a life-giver. Without an occasional fire, all the trees mature at the same time, limiting the diversity of food and wildlife. This does not mean that all forest fires are good. Nature has ways of regulating its own growth, and humans should think twice before interfering, either by setting fires or by putting out those that occur naturally.

Plant communities change and mature at different times in a natural process called succession. For example, the flowers and grasses of an open meadow may be replaced eventually by young trees. As the trees mature, less and less light reaches the ground, and fewer kinds of plants grow there. That means that fewer kinds of animals can find food. Insects attack the oldest trees, causing them to fall and become fuel, waiting for a fire to start the process anew. If this process is stopped, the floors of old forests collect huge amounts of brush and dead trees, disease spreads, the food supply is limited, and diversity of wildlife is limited.

Yellowstone researchers studied tree rings and fire scars on lodgepole pines and discovered that major blazes had occurred every 200 to 400 years. After a fire, the forest floor becomes a lush, colorful carpet of tender grasses, wild berries, and flowers. Heat is absorbed into the black soil, so plants grow faster. In a matter of hours, a tree destroyed is reduced to chemicals and ash rich in life-giving nitrogen, calcium, potassium, and phosphorus. Rabbits, mice, and other small animals move in to enjoy the banquet. These animals, in turn, attract hungry coyotes and owls. As new bushes and plants grow larger, moose and elk move in.

These benefits could not be ignored. With the release of the Leopold Report in 1963, park management became more fire-friendly. By 1972, Yellowstone was one of a few national parks to implement a "natural fire" policy—the policy

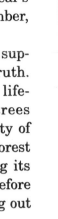

Smokey the Bear was successfully used to convince the public that forests and fires didn't mix.

It doesn't take too long after a forest fire for new plant growth to emerge, renewing a mature forest with new growth.

# SPECIAL ADAPTATIONS

Some plants in Yellowstone developed special features because of fire. As lodgepole pines grow, their lower branches fall off, leaving the green treetops, called the canopy, high off the ground. Unlike with spruce and fir trees, whose branches often touch the ground, fire cannot spread up a lodgepole trunk very easily.

On the other hand, lodgepoles often need fire to release their seeds, which are bound in cones (left) by a waxy substance called resin. Fire softens this natural adhesive and opens the cones (right). As many as 300,000 new trees may sprout up on a single acre after a fire.

In Yellowstone, however, the lodgepole has adapted a little differently. Scientists discovered most Yellowstone lodgepole cones now release their seeds without fire. Many cones open without fire, although a few of the resin-sealed cones are produced on each tree.

followed in 1988. Fires caused by lightning were allowed to burn as long as people, buildings, endangered species, special park features, and prehistoric Native American sites were not threatened. Fires caused by humans would still be fought. Controlled fires, called "prescribed burns," would be started when necessary to clear areas with too much debris.

## A Natural Inferno

The summer of 1988 started like any other in Yellowstone country with one exception—the usual heavy rainstorms didn't come. Lightning strikes are common at this time of year, but most fires go out after burning several hundred acres. In the 16 years since the natural fire policy was adopted, only 34,175 acres (13,830 ha) had burned in the park from natural causes.

Perhaps there was some lack of concern that summer. Because the park elevation averages 8,000 feet (2,438 m), wet snow blankets forests most of the year, leaving them almost too wet to even catch fire. Even though 1988 was exceptionally dry—the driest year in 50 years—experts predicted that no more than 45,000 acres (18,211 ha) would be touched. They didn't know that July and August would see no moisture at all. This drought lowered the moisture content of forest debris to a very low 2 to 3 percent. The lumber we use to build houses contains 12 percent moisture even after being dried.

On June 14, when lightning struck in the Absaroka-Beartooth Wilderness northeast of the park, no one expected an inferno. Experience had taught that these fires usually go out on their own. This year, however, was a totally new experience. Lightning flashed all over the park like a giant octopus whose teasing tentacles hit Greater Yellowstone at will. By the end of July, 13 major wildfires,

The Clover (below) and Mist fires in the northeast portion of the park merged on July 22, the same day the North Fork fire was started in Targhee National Forest by careless woodcutters.

all burning at different speeds and in different directions, created an inferno that was completely out of control. Park personnel and citizens living in communities outside the park began to clamor for something to be done. The natural burn policy was abandoned on July 17.

All efforts to contain the blazes failed, however. Wind was the biggest factor. That summer, six dry storms passed through, packing winds up to 70 miles per hour (113 kph). These winds carried apple-sized embers as far as 2 miles (3.2 km) ahead of fire lines, where they started new fires. This phenomenon, called "spotting," could not be controlled. Fires even jumped the Grand Canyon of the Yellowstone River, leaving firefighters behind.

Over 150,000 acres (60,704 ha) were torched in a single day. August 20, 1988, was called "Black Saturday." Huge, ominous smoke clouds filled the summer skies. Tornadolike firestorms with violent winds and walls of flame as high as 300 feet (91 m) ravaged the landscape. Boulders exploded. Trees were ripped from the ground like toothpicks. Park personnel called it "fire behavior out of the Twilight Zone."

Nature began snuffing the fires out the second week of September. A light snow covered the entire park, followed by rain several days later. The flames continued, but the fury was gone. An almost festive atmosphere enveloped the towns near Yellowstone. Radio stations broadcast Christmas music, hoping to coax more snow from the heavens. By October, cooperative storms had extinguished the inferno. Firefighters had made no real difference.

The fires of 1988 were difficult to fight because of strong winds. The flames also didn't die down at night.

The map shows areas of the Yellowstone region burned during the fires of 1988. The names of the major fires are shown next to the red triangles.

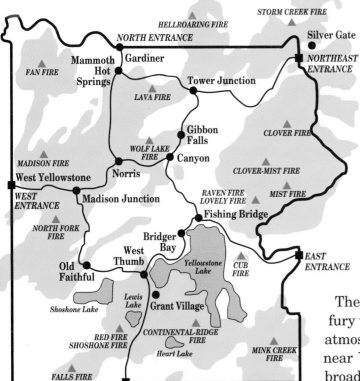

## The Good and the Bad

Satellite photos of Greater Yellowstone showed that 706,277 acres (285,823 ha) within the park and 285,002 acres (115,337 ha) in the adjacent national forests had been burned. The largest fires were monsters. The perimeter of the North Fork fire alone surrounded 504,025 acres (203,974 ha).

A total of 25,000 firefighters and 90 aircraft battled the blazes at a total cost of $111,377,623, or $1.5 million each firefighting day. And 1,000 miles (1,609 km) of fire lines, trenches that a fire cannot cross, were dug.

Most of the affected burn areas looked like patchwork crazy quilts, with different sizes and shapes of brown and black next to pieces of untouched green. Spotting had caused the uneven patterns and uneven burn. For example, the Fan Fire consumed about one-third of the area within its boundaries, while the Madison River, Lava Creek, and Firehole fires burned about three-fourths of the area within their perimeters. Some fires, such as Wolf Creek, burned close to the ground quite slowly, turning the dead forest debris into a rich cover of ash.

In the final analysis, only about 22,000 acres (8,903 ha)—less than one percent of the total—were burned by a "hot" fire, a blaze so hot that the ground is sterilized, killing seeds, bulbs, and any nutrients. Because the fires had passed through some areas rapidly, only the canopy (tops of trees) in half the fire regions burned. The damage was not as bad as the media reported.

Most animals simply got out of the way as the fire passed. Bison wandered back into burned-over land to lick nutrient-rich ashes before the ground was cold. Some elk grazed within 50 feet (15 m) of

Elk came back into burned areas almost as soon as the fires had passed.

A patchwork of forest areas were burned during the 1988 fires. This picture shows the view from Mt. Washburn after the fires were out.

## CAUSED BY CARELESSNESS

All but three of Yellowstone's major fires in 1988 were started by lightning, but the worst and most publicized fire—the North Fork—was due to human carelessness. Four men entered Targhee National Forest west of the park on July 22 to cut firewood. During an innocent smoke break, the men dropped their cigarette butts in a paper-dry forest. Within hours the fire was out of control. The Old Faithful area was threatened by the North Fork fire. Flames came within 0.75 miles (1.2 km) of Old Faithful Geyser. Sprinklers were quickly installed to save the historic inn, and people were evacuated before the firestorm swept across the area. Sixteen cabins were destroyed, but the Old Faithful Inn stood. When it was all over, the woodcutters were convicted of a simple misdemeanor. Forty million dollars were spent trying to contain this one blaze, and over 500,000 acres (202,345 ha) were affected. It was the largest single fire in the park's history.

the flaming forests, totally unconcerned. But the real consequences of fire affect animals after the fires are gone.

Because the drought was so severe prior to the fires, and the food supply was not as good as usual, thinner elk and bison faced the 1988-1989 winter. About 9,000 elk died, killed by either starvation or by hunters who legally harvested the animals once they were outside park boundaries. And when the northern herd of 900 bison left the park looking for winter range, they did not fare well. Hunters killed 569 of these animals in what some conservation groups called a "slaughter."

Death in nature is not a bad thing. Dead elk and bison provide meals for scavengers such as bears, eagles, and coyotes. In addition, plant communities—struck by both drought and fire—are better able to support the remaining animals. But humans don't like to see animals in "trouble." After the fires, criticism was rampant because the park service had no intention of providing supplemental feeding. At the town of Gardiner, Montana, pro-feeding sentiment ran high. A poem, tacked to park headquarter doors and bulletin boards, expressed this feeling:

In nature, dead animals provide food for scavengers. A mule deer carcass provides a meal for a black bear (below).

> Here's to your government who let the park burn,
> So rangeland grasses took a wrong turn.
> The animals are starving leaving the park,
> Heading to Gardiner for edible tree bark.
> If you have sympathy and like to donate,
> Put money in this fund before it's too late.

Humans don't trust nature to repair itself and take care of its own, but it does, and it has. Most of the blackened areas are now full of tiny young pine trees, carpets of green grasses, wildflowers, and thick bushes. Elk and bison are healthy and fat. Some visitors think, however, that the forest of tall black trees, standing guard over the lush, green renewal, is still a national shame. They believe the natural burn policy was a complete failure. The *Wall Street Journal* called Yellowstone Park a "smoke-blackened ruin because of failed federal forest-management policies."

Since the 1988 fire, some modifications have been made in the fire policy. Naturally-caused fires are still allowed to burn, but park personnel are paying more attention to other conditions so that they may better access current weather conditions and the availability of fire-fighting resources.

In the end, what most people think is not that important. Yellowstone is alive and thriving now. However, there are still 1 million acres (404,690 ha) of old-growth lodgepole pine alive and vulnerable to a fire such as the one that occurred in 1988. Under the same climatic conditions, history will repeat itself in spite of any government policy.

The picture above was taken in October of 1988. By July of 1989, the same burned region had new green growth (bottom) and was recovering from the fires of the previous summer.

# Chapter Six

# Managing for the Future

Rainbow trout spawn in the Firehole River in December, when the temperature of its hot water sinks to 50°F (10°C). Despite the frigid winter landscape, the fish are safe in their watery home. Cross-country skiers pass by, not interested in what's happening in the river. Some are after a photo of the majestic elk and frost-covered bison nearby. Skiers can go anywhere in the park, and they like to come as close to these animals as possible, often startling the animals and causing them to run. This seems harmless enough, but most skiers do not realize that an animal on the run during a Yellowstone winter is using precious energy. Unnecessary exertion might mean death before spring can bring a more plentiful food supply.

Visitors didn't start spending winter in the park until the late 1960s. Before snowmobilers, skiers, and sleighs broke the white silence, Yellowstone got a well-deserved rest blanketed in refreshing snow and subzero temperatures. That's not the case anymore, as 100,000 winter visitors, eager to invade a new frontier, stream into the park. Roads carry about 600 snowmobiles each day, along with animals who find the roads an easy way to travel. Snowmobiles are limited to 45 miles per hour (72 kph) and must stay on the pavement. Skiers, however, can travel anywhere. Both skiers and snowmobilers present new management problems in the park. Managers have to decide how many can be accommodated and predict their effect on wildlife.

Yellowstone was established for the enjoyment of the people, and recreational use of its lands is a high priority. But it was also established as a nature preserve, where animals and plants would be protected. As some groups push for opening the park and surrounding lands to new kinds of year-round recreation, other groups push just as hard to stop, stand back, and examine the consequences of more visitors and more development.

In the midst of opposing arguments, everyone needs to remember that Yellowstone National Park is not an island but the center of an 18-million-acre

The number of winter visitors to Yellowstone increases each year. They pose new management problems.

(7,284,420-ha) temperate zone region, known as Greater Yellowstone Ecosystem. What happens outside the park boundaries is just as important as what happens inside. Nature knows no borders. Many conservationists consider this ecosystem the last great pristine temperate-zone ecosystem left on Earth. They think it is a place worth saving at any cost.

## Integrated Management

Seven national forests, three wildlife refuges, and several wilderness areas surround Yellowstone National Park. These lands around the park are managed by over 30 different federal and state agencies. Various activities, such as mining, logging, or grazing, are allowed in different jurisdictions. For example, most of the national forests are governed by a multi-use policy. Grazing, mining, logging, and gas and oil drilling are allowed.

Unlike national forests, wilderness areas, which cover about one-third of Greater Yellowstone, are protected by the National Wilderness System. Commercial grazing is allowed, but logging, mining, road building or motorized vehicles are not. In the past, commercial interests usually won out, but today there is more emphasis on how any of these multi-use activities will affect the plant and animal life in the entire Greater Yellowstone Ecosystem.

Today, park officials are concerned with providing safe recreation for visitors and in conserving and protecting the wildlife within park boundaries

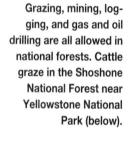

Grazing, mining, logging, and gas and oil drilling are all allowed in national forests. Cattle graze in the Shoshone National Forest near Yellowstone National Park (below).

# DISCOVERING GRIZZLY BEARS

On August 27, 1993, the Grizzly Discovery Center (GDC) opened at West Yellowstone, Montana. This 1-acre grizzly-habitat area is the first part of a large $50-million commercial development called Grizzly Park. Lewis Robinson III and the Firehole Land Corporation are developing the site, which will eventually include several grizzly-habitat areas, a hotel, restaurants, stores, and a large theater. Some conservationists are concerned that the center might give people the idea that "...Yellowstone is a glorified zoo." Robinson believes, however, that the development will allow Yellowstone's tourists to realize the dream of actually seeing a live grizzly bear in its natural habitat—behind a 12-foot-high fence.

GDC's original plan was to house so-called "nuisance" bears from the park—those who can't stay away from in-park developments. Every year, about six grizzlies are captured by park rangers and released into the backcountry. They are given only three chances to change their behavior before they are killed or placed in zoos. To date, however, none of the Grizzly Center's five bears are from the lower 48 states.

The GDC is affiliated with the International Grizzly Fund , also located on the property. Part of all GDC revenues is donated to the fund which will be used to help preserve grizzly bears in their natural habitat.

This area of Lewis and Clark National Forest in Montana is part of the Bear Tree Project. The forest service is trying to encourage the regeneration of buffalo berry bushes on this site. The bushes are essential forage for the grizzly bear.

through natural management. But Yellowstone's mammals do not recognize park boundaries, so they often come in contact with ranchers and businessmen outside the park, where the presence of wild animals can interfere with human activities.

The Greater Yellowstone Coalition, a group of about 100 organizations, was formed in 1983 to promote the idea of cooperation or integrated management of the whole ecosystem. This means that land-use decisions should be made considering the the animals and plants that live there. Originally motivated by a desire to protect grizzly bear habitat, the group is a watchdog for any activity that might drastically change the ecosystem. The coalition is cooperating with ranchers and developers to protect the entire ecosystem. Government workers and conservation groups are all working hard to implement an ecosystem management policy that is enforceable. Trying to accommodate everyone's interests, needs and rights under the law without hurting the park is always a challenge.

## Inside the Park

Although only about two percent of the land within the park is developed, that development must be done carefully. To accommodate visitors, over 1,200 miles (1,930 km) of trails and over 2,000 buildings have been constructed. Almost 370 miles

(595 km) of paved roads, 24 water systems, 30 sewer systems, 10 electric generating systems, and thousands of campsites provide human comforts.

Some facilities have brought humans and wildlife in close contact. For example, the Fishing Bridge area is located where the Yellowstone River flows from Yellowstone Lake in prime grizzly bear habitat. Cutthroat trout spawn here, and grizzly bears eat them. In the 1970s and 1980s, a visitor complex called Grant Village was built on the west shore of Yellowstone Lake. Conservationists hoped this new development would take the place of the development near Fishing Bridge, leaving the area for grizzlies and reducing the risk of human encounters with the bears. The park service did remove some cabins, campgrounds, and other facilities, but pressure from various groups at Fishing Bridge forced the park service to leave a trailer park with 353 sites open.

## Harvesting Timber

If you saw the western boundary of Yellowstone National Park from high above Earth, you would see a distinct line in most places where loggers harvested trees right up to the park border. On the park side stands thick forest; on the other side, treeless land. The Gallatin and Targhee National Forests are heavily logged by a method called clear-cutting, which means that all the trees are cut down at once.

Logging can be harmful because it can change habitat. Once the trees are gone there is less vegetation to hold the soil in place, and soil is washed away into waterways. Roads built for access to forests can

Housing developments outside the park also pose threats to wildlife habitat. About 20 percent of the land in the ecosystem is privately owned. Much of that land is along waterways or other critical wildlife habitat that probably shouldn't be developed.

Some clear-cut areas in Targhee National Forest have been replanted, but it will take years for the trees to grow. Most often, the habitat will not be quite the same as it was before clear-cutting.

Small logging operations, such as this family post company, compete with larger companies for the timber in the Yellowstone Ecosytem.

break up wildlife habitat and allow easier access for poachers. In the Gallatin and Targhee national forests, access roads dissect the land. In the last few years, few female grizzly bears or cubs have been seen in areas west of the park where clear-cutting and road building have been so extensive.

Some forested land is privately owned. In the summer of 1992, the Plum Creek Lumber Company sold 164,000 acres (66,475 ha) to Big Sky Lumber. The new owner plans to build exclusive homes on some of the land and to supply raw lumber to Louisiana Pacific Corporation with the rest. The Nature Conservancy and other conservation groups are trying to buy key portions of this parcel to preserve critical elk range.

## Mining

Mining can scar the land and may produce waste that contaminates water above and below ground. Wildlife habitat can be changed in the process, and reclaiming the land probably won't create the same kind or quality of habitat that existed before.

Platinum, gold, silver, copper, and other minerals are found in the mountains surrounding Yellowstone. A Canadian corporation, Noranda Minerals, plans to mine gold and silver just 2 miles (3.2 km) from the park's northeast boundary, near Cooke City, Montana. This is an area of whitebark pine forests where grizzly bears come to eat pine nuts, a critical food supply for these animals before they hibernate. The company is still involved in getting permits, but exploratory work has begun.

The Stillwater Mining Company is digging for platinum near the northern boundary in Custer National Forest. Since 1987, this precious metal, previously imported, has made millions of dollars for the mining company, selling for about $500 an ounce (28.3 g). Some conservationists fear not only harm to the beauty of the landscape but also the effects of runoff from the mining site. The runoff can contain chemicals and other harmful substances that might contaminate the water supply.

Besides loss of grizzly bear habitat and possible water quality problems, the Noranda mine will probably be a blemish on the beautiful scenery along the Beartooth Highway.

## Drilling Near Yellowstone

After the energy shortages of the 1970s, developers looked to the Greater Yellowstone area for new sources of energy. Drilling deep into the ground outside the park has people worried about the fragile thermal areas inside the park. With the park's delicate underground plumbing system, drilling might cause heat patterns and water flow to change.

In 1992, the Church Universal and Triumphant, led by Elizabeth Clare Prophet, drilled a well in a hot spring region near Corwin Springs, Montana. The group wanted water to fill a swimming pool on their 33,000-acre (13,355-ha) complex just north of Yellowstone's boundaries. Alarmed by possible consequences to the thermal regions inside the park, the U.S. Congress was able to temporarily stop the group from any further drilling.

Federal protection is probably needed to protect Yellowstone's thermal features. The Old Faithful Protection Act, now stalled in the U.S. Senate, would provide the legal muscle that conservation groups want. The bill would permanently stop drilling within a 15-mile (24-km) buffer zone next to the park and within the Corwin Springs Known Geothermal Resource Area, where the Church Universal drilled. But personal property rights, guaranteed by the U.S. Constitution, must also be considered when finding a workable and fair solution.

Drilling near Yellowstone may cause damage to the delicate underground plumbing system of the thermal regions. This oil rig is located in the Targhee National Forest just outside the park.

## A Place So Special

If some changes in Greater Yellowstone are not slowed, future visitors to the park may never see all its wonders. Those who visit the park today do not find some of the wildlife Theodore Roosevelt saw in the early 1900s—packs of gray wolves and a large, healthy beaver population.

A policy of natural management is being pursued inside the park, but this alone will not remedy park problems because there are also challenges outside the park. Nature's processes and creatures do not recognize lines drawn by humans. As we become more educated about the entire Greater Yellowstone Ecosystem, we will realize that the center of it all, Yellowstone National Park, cannot survive as an island.

Citizens of the world have long recognized the unique place Yellowstone National Park occupies on the planet. The Earl of Dunraven came from England to visit the newly created national park and published a book about his

Located along the Gibbon River Canyon, Gibbon Falls is one of many beautiful waterfalls in the park.

A lone bull elk stands in the water of the Gibbon River.

trip, *The Great Divide*, in 1876. Thrilled by what he saw, he wrote: "All honor then to the United States for having bequeathed as a free gift to man the beauties and curiosities of Wonderland. It is an act worthy of a great nation, and she will have her reward in the praise of the present army of tourists no less than in the thanks of the generations to come."

The United Nations declared the park a Biosphere Reserve in 1976, the first one in the United States. In 1978, it was designated a World Heritage Site. These designations are important, but the United States is the only nation that can protect the park and the lands surrounding it. Balancing the demands of nature and the demands of development and tourism is not an easy task. We have enough zoological gardens but few places quite so special. The solitude found in Yellowstone's wildness and the lessons we can learn from its ecosystem are an invaluable resource to all Earth's people.

Blue sky reflected by Emerald Spring's clear water and yellow from its sulfur-lined basin combine to make a beautiful green. Located in Norris Geyser Basin, the water is always near the boiling point.

# GLOSSARY

**andesite** – a gray, fine-grained volcanic rock.

**caldera** – the bowllike depression formed when a volcano erupts and then collapses inward as it cools.

**carnivores** – meat-eating animals.

**chemosynthesis** – a process whereby an organism uses chemicals instead of sunlight to produce energy. The chemical reactions are caused by the synthesis of organic substances.

**ecosystem** – a group of interacting organisms in a particular physical environment.

**firestorm** – an uncontrollable, violent fire that develops tornadolike winds and intense heat.

**flashing** – instantaneous and violent boiling of water when pressure is reduced.

**fumarole** – vent or opening in the ground through which superheated steam escapes.

**geothermal** – refers to heat from the interior of the Earth. Geothermal areas are usually in regions of volcanic activity. Some geothermal features are geysers, hot springs, fumaroles, and mud pots.

**geyser** – a hot spring that erupts at intervals, shooting steam and water into the air.

**geyserite** – a rock-like silica-rich substance dissolved in water. This substance lines geyser plumbing systems. It is deposited aboveground to form cones and covers the surface of geyser basins. It is also called sinter.

**Greater Yellowstone Ecosystem** – an 18-million-acre (7.2-million-ha) temperate-zone ecosystem with Yellowstone National Park at the center. Includes seven national forests, three national wildlife refuges, and Grand Teton National Park.

**herbivores** – plant-eating animals.

**hot fire** – a fire that is so destructive it sterilizes the soil, killing all seeds and organic material.

**hot spring** – a pool of water, often characterized by beautiful colors, heated from an underground heat source.

**magma** – hot, liquid rock deep below the Earth's surface.

**mud pot** – a type of hot spring with a limited water supply. Hot steam containing sulfuric acid breaks down rock, forming thick, boiling clay.

**natural management** – a type of management in which natural processes are allowed to take their course without human interference.

**omnivores** – animals that eat both plants and other animals.

**plateau** – relatively flat land region above sea level.

**predators** – animals that hunt and kill other animals for food.

**prey** – animals, usually plant-eaters, that are killed by other animals as food.

**rhyolite** – a type of volcanic rock.

**scavengers** – animals that eat the meat of dead animals.

**spotting** – a phenomenon during a fire in which embers blown by strong winds start fires outside the main fire's perimeter.

**succession** – a natural process in which plant communities change and mature at different times.

**travertine** – dissolved limestone called calcium carbonate deposited aboveground.

**ungulates** – hoofed animals.

# FOR MORE INFORMATION

**Books**

Fishbein, Seymour L. *Yellowstone Country: The Enduring Wonder*. Washington, D.C.: Special Publications Division, National Geographic Society, 1989.

Haines, A.L. *Osborne Russell's Journal of a Trapper*. Lincoln, Nebr.: University of Nebraska, 1955.

Schullery, Paul. *The Bears of Yellowstone*. Worland, Wyo.: High Plains Publishing, 1992.

Simpson, Ross W. *The Fires of '88*. Helena, Mont.: American Geographic, 1989.

Sutton, Ann and Myron. *Yellowstone: A Century of the Wilderness Idea*. New York: Macmillan, Yellowstone Library and Museum Association, 1972.

Wuerthner, George. *Yellowstone: A Visitor's Companion*. Harrisburg, Pa.: Stackpole, 1992.

**Videos**

*The Complete Yellowstone, A Four-Season Tour*, FHFC.

*Geysers of Yellowstone*, FHFC.

*Story of Yellowstone National Park*, Questar Productions, 1991.

*Survivors of the Fire: Yellowstone's Elk*, Grunko Films.

*Yellowstone National Park*, Bryce/Zion National Parks series, Wilderness Video, 1987.

# INDEX